Free at Last

7 Spiritual Tools

for conquering your addictions

by Pat MacEnulty

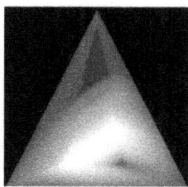

PRISM LIGHT
PRESS

ISBN 978-0-9830357-4-9

Published by
Prism Light Press
PO Box 625, Tallahassee, FL 32302
www.prismlightpress.com

Manufactured in the United States of America.

Table of Contents

For those who love us anyway

Introduction

Our bodies are the living vehicles for Spirit. They are the good and faithful servants of our souls. If we saw someone abusing a horse, we would call the police and have it stopped. However, we see people abusing their bodies on a daily basis and we feel powerless to do anything. But no one can make another person conquer his or her addiction.

So how does someone give up an addiction? It seems impossible. When I was a young woman, the idea of a day without drugs was a dark prospect indeed. I lived for heroin, methadone, cocaine, whatever was available. I was not living for myself, and I certainly wasn't on track to a purposeful, meaningful life. You may say, "Well, I'm not into anything like that. I smoke cigarettes, and that isn't nearly as bad." But there is no doubt that cigarette smoking is dangerous and causes serious and often fatal diseases. Nicotine addiction is so insidious that I have seen cigarette smokers become socially isolated because they can't give up their habits to ease someone else's discomfort. Food addicts and people with eating disorders usually know that their addiction can be deadly and at the very least can destroy their self-esteem. And then there are sex addicts who endanger their relationships, put themselves at risk of contracting sexually transmitted diseases, and slowly erode their reputations through their addictive behaviors.

All of these substances and behaviors actually have a useful place in the pantheon of human experience. Drugs help ease pain in times of physical trauma, a glass of wine is a wonderful way to relax after a hard day of work, and tobacco is a part of the spiritual tradition of many Native American tribes. We have to eat, and life without sex would be less than fulfilling for most of us and would eventually lead to the end of the human race.

However, addicts—whether they are addicted to cigarettes, alcohol, drugs, food, gambling, the Internet or sex—are not in control of their lives. We all have a unique talent, a unique purpose in this life. But the addict's purpose in life becomes perverted by addiction. It may be that the addiction is part of her spiritual journey but if that is the case, then its purpose is to lead her to a more healthy life and the sooner, the better.

Addiction is not a disease in the sense that cancer or multiple sclerosis is a disease. It is the result of our choices. Because it is the result of our choices, we can make other choices. Kicking an addiction is simple, but it's not easy. In fact, it may seem downright impossible. But it isn't. If it were, there would not be so many of us who have done it.

According to a report by National Public Radio; "Cheap and very pure heroin is creating a growing addiction crisis across America. Heroin -- much of it from Colombia -- is replacing crack cocaine as the drug of choice, particularly among the young. In Massachusetts, for example, more than 4 percent of high school boys report having used heroin. . . . Heroin is pure enough to snort these days, and younger people are getting into it. In the Boston area, the number of 18 and 19 year olds seeking emergency-room treatment related to heroin use doubled between 2000 and 2002."

But it's not just hard drugs that are the problem. Cigarettes, dope, bulimia and anorexia, overeating, booze, sex, video games, violent television, gambling—indulging in any of these behaviors or substances to excess can become an addiction that eventually wrests control of our lives and perverts our true purpose. Addicts are never able to truly speak for themselves. Instead the addiction is always speaking through them. If we cannot be authentic, then we cannot experience the divinity within, and that is tragic.

The Origin of the Tools

While this book speaks specifically toward addicts and their families, the tools described here can be used by anyone who is in need of spiritual direction. They can be used to heal depression, unhealthy relationships, and the everyday problems that most of us confront.

I have put together these tools from my own experience as a former heroin addict and cocaine user. The people I have known who have successfully moved from addictive lives to lives of fulfillment and purpose have also used one or more of these tools. These tools are not steps to be done once and then forgotten about. They are habits of life. While I am suggesting a certain order, this may not necessarily be the order that you use. It may be that you have already discovered one or two of these tools for yourself and that is why you are reading the book.

The foundational teachings for this book include *A Course in Miracles, The Four Agreements* by Don Miguel Ruiz, *The Path of Prayer: Reflections on Prayer and True Stories of How It Affects Our Lives* by Sophy Burnham, *The Science of Mind* by Ernest Holmes, and *The Holy Bible, Standard Revised Edition*. I also incorporate the practical teachings of Sadhguru, Deepak Chopra, Joan Borysenko, Rumi and other spiritual teachers.

The truth is that it is easy to get clean, to kick the habit, to get the monkey off your back. The hard part, as most of us know, is staying clean. The physical withdrawal may be extremely painful and grueling. And yet it is short-lived. The emotional, psychological hook is the one we just can't seem to extract. And so you'll find that these chapters don't just deal with physical addiction. The tools are to help you change your life so that once you get clean, you can stay that way. Will you fall? Perhaps. I did. It was a hard fall, but I didn't stay down. I had the spiritual resources to get back on my feet, dust myself off and move forward into a fulfilling life.

Who needs to read this book? Addicts of all persuasions, their family members, ministers and church groups, mental health practitioners, teachers and anyone involved in recovery. If you are sincerely looking for help, then you can conquer your addictions. Here's to your new life.

Free At Last

*Many names in the case studies have been
changed to protect the privacy of the people
who have chosen to share their stories.
The facts of the stories remain unaltered.*

ONE
The Spiritual Meaning of Addiction

In the animated movie, *Spirited Away*, there is a scene in which a little girl's parents sit down in a restaurant and begin gobbling up all the food even though there is no one else there—not a single waiter, cook or cashier. They start eating and they can't stop. Frustrated by their single-minded attention on the food, the little girl wanders away. When she comes back, they are still gobbling away, but they no longer look like her parents. Instead they have become giant pigs.

That image resonates as a familiar idea in our world. We live in a culture that encourages addictive behaviors. We are indoctrinated into the mighty culture of consumption from the time we are toddlers: *Eat, buy, drink, buy, drive, buy, wear, buy, buy, buy.* These are the messages we hear and see on a daily basis. No wonder so many people are on some kind of antidepressant. We do what the culture promises will bring us happiness, but it doesn't work. No amount of the right kind of cars, beer, antiperspirant, yogurt, or whatever will make us happy.

On a larger scale, we can see that our political and business leaders have become addicted to power and money. Corporations engage in mass swindles and no one seems to mind. In fact, the government allows and even aids them in these swindles, while children in America and around the world go hungry. The gap between the rich and poor grows ever wider, while some of us wonder, just how much money do the rich really need? How many mansions, yachts, trips around the world and wardrobes worth tens of thousands of dollars are necessary to make them happy?

It's enough to make many of us do whatever we can to dull the pain and blind ourselves to things that are out of our control. And so we start on a strange and self-destructive course that ends up in addiction.

It's easy to find reasons for an individual's addictive behaviors. There are the larger societal concerns and pressures described above. And there are the personal traumas and tragedies that drive some of us to seek annihilation—abusive parents, sexual abuse, poverty and oppression, accidents, violence. But it ultimately comes down to a choice. Before any behavior becomes an addiction, it starts out as a conscious choice. We choose to light that cigarette, binge on that chocolate cake, wander into that porno store, pour that vodka into a glass or stick that crack pipe in our mouths.

Many would like to place the blame on the society, the addicts' parents or on the addicts themselves, but at some point, we must stop the blame and guilt game. An addict becomes an addict because at the time that seemed like a viable antidote to pain and unhappiness.

Spiritually speaking, addiction is simply attachment taken to an extreme. And attachment stems from desire. We have myriad desires for a wide variety of conditions and things from sexual desire to desires for luxury items, fame, adventure and attention.

Desire can be a wonderful motivation for us to achieve great things. Desire can also be a trap if we don't realize that all desires stem from one desire: the desire to experience our unity with the Divine. If we can stop and look at all our desires for outward things as an expression of this basic inward desire, then we gain perspective on our desires, on our attachments to those things which seem to satisfy those desires and on those addictions that are merely our attachments taken to an extreme.

Case Study, Kenneth: Kenneth, a teacher at a community college, had been in a relationship with his partner, Tom, for three years before Tom discovered that Kenneth was addicted to pornography. Kenneth explains:

I couldn't help myself. I would look at internet porn for hours. Instead of devoting time to my partner, I was completely captivated by these images. Finally, just looking at images wasn't enough, and so I went out cruising. I probably had thirty different sexual encounters behind Tom's back. When he finally asked me about it, I just let it all spill out. I didn't even know the names of these guys. Tom was so hurt. He left me, and I was completely shattered. I had lost the best relationship I ever had. No, I had thrown it away. So I had to ask myself why? And I finally began to see that I didn't feel worthy of love. I mean, I grew up in the Deep South, and all my life I was told that it was a sin to be gay and that I was going to hell. Instead of facing the truth I drowned out my feelings of inadequacy through these casual sexual encounters.

Well, I stopped blaming my parents for not understanding me. I forgave my father. I realized that if I wanted love in my life I was going to have to admit that I was worthy of it—of real love. I began going to a therapist. I stopped going out to clubs every weekend. I knew I had to take responsibility for my actions. I had to accept myself and love myself. Eventually, Tom came back. We're taking it "one day at a time" and so far, it's working.

Make it work for you:

This is an exercise in understanding and releasing your past. The reason this is the first exercise is because I want you to do it once and then put it behind you. It does no good to dwell on our past mistakes or our terrible childhood traumas. They happened. However, it is crucial to recognize those actions we think of as mistakes or bad choices, to acknowledge them, and then to think about how we might make different choices in the future. Spend some time with this exercise, cry if you need to, but remember it is only for your eyes. When you are done, burn it, release it, imagine all your fears and sorrows disappearing in a puff of smoke. So get out your journal or a sheet a paper and your pen and answer the following questions:

- What was the first choice you made that led to an addictive behavior?

- What other choices might you have made?

- What have you learned from the choice you did make?

- Why do you think you made that particular choice?

- If people hurt you in the past, why do you think they did that?

- What desires led you to this addictive behavior?

- What is it that you truly desire?

- What choices are you making today to obtain that desire?

- Are you willing to accept the possibility that there is a solution to your problems?

- Are you willing to believe that everything you did, every mistake you made, every failure you felt, was leading you to this moment?

Now below your answers, write: "I am willing to honor and release my past. I am completely free. I am new wine in a new wineskin."

TWO
Ask Spirit for Help, Listen for the Answer

There is a reason why the most well-known step of the 12-step programs is the third step: give your problems to your higher power. Notice that it is YOUR higher power, not my higher power. Your higher power is not some authority outside of yourself. It is a power that is yours to use any time you are willing to claim it.

Why do you need this higher power? Why not just stop doing whatever unhealthy behavior you're doing? Because the problems that caused you to drink that six-pack or smoke that cigarette or inject that narcotic are still there. And once your medication is gone, then you have to deal with it. To do that you have to love yourself. To love yourself, you must know that you are divine. To know your own divinity, you must commune with Spirit.

You may call this higher power Spirit, God, the Christ Consciousness, Creator, the I am, Divine Intelligence, Love, Brahman, Allah, Henry, or any number of names. It is that which is there for you when all else has failed. It is that which is your inner most being.

When you are in your most desperate hour, that is when you turn within and say, "Please help me." Because God's ear is in your own heart, your cry is always heard. As you develop your prayer habits, you will learn that you do not need to ask for help. You can thank God or Spirit or your Higher Power for having already helped you. Jesus said, "Ask, believing that you have already received."

But when we are struggling with the pain underneath our addictions, it may be difficult to believe that we are worthy of Grace. As Sophy Burnham says in her book, *A Path to Prayer*: "Some people try to push the painful situation into submission by drive and hard work, while others take to alcohol or drugs, in an effort either to dull the unwanted sensations or else to vault over them into some exalted happy state (using spirits to reach the spiritual), and for a short time this may work." I remember a time in my life when I naively thought that drugs would help me find God. Well, they did in a roundabout way, but there were easier and quicker routes I could have taken.

When all our running and dodging stops working, when the pain we feel at the emotional level becomes a knife twisting in our gut, that is when we cry out. The hard shell of our heart breaks open and we allow the Presence to awaken within us.

For addicts especially there are useful, time-honored prayers. The Serenity Prayer has helped millions of alcoholics and their family members make it "one day at a time." I love the Lord's Prayer, though I sometimes reword it—especially if I'm feeling sensitive about "father" issues. There's a wonderful line in that prayer—"lead us not into temptation." Sometimes we might feel we're not really strong enough to withstand temptation. I know when I was ready to quit cocaine, I still didn't quite have the power to say "no" if it was in front of me. So I prayed for the temptation to go away. I didn't automatically throw off my desire for the drug, but slowly it became less and less a part of my life until one day I realized it had been years since I'd done any cocaine—and the desire was truly gone.

Jesus offers us another way to confront temptation—the same way he did when he was in the desert. He said, "Get thee behind me, Satan." Satan can be thought of as that part of ourselves, that weakness, which would destroy us. I love the fact that Jesus was tempted. If there hadn't been some small part of him that urged him to do what he did not want to do, then it wouldn't have been a temptation. Jesus, as a human, was able to show us how to deal with it.

Developing the Voice of Self-Preservation

In the bitter cold days of winter, I am always astounded to see a few miserable souls standing outside of the academic building at the university where I teach, smoking their poor lungs out. Don't they have that voice in their heads that asks, "What the hell am I doing out here in the freezing cold?" Is that voice simply missing? Then with sudden clarity I look back into my own past and remember when not only did I not have that self-love, self-preservation voice, I heard a much stronger and much more insidious voice: the voice of addiction.

When I was addicted to narcotics, I would find myself in incredibly dangerous and degrading situations over and over again -- in a car trying to outrun police; in a motel room with a paranoid, coked-up stranger; face down on the pavement in the freezing rain with guns pointed at my head. My self-preservation voice was silent, muted by a force of destructive will.

I suppose that's why one of the truisms of addiction is that an addict must hit "bottom" before changing. It must be that at some point when you are staring at the abyss your soul is about to tumble into, self-preservation kicks in and you hear a voice that says, "What am I doing? I deserve better than this." This voice I believe is the voice of our primary selves -- our god-selves, the divinity within. The Bible refers to a "still, small voice." We all have it.

I can't pinpoint the exact moment when that voice became activated in my head. But I know that along with self-preservation, I developed a revulsion for the things that were trying to suck me into the mire. Non-addicts generally feel revulsion for the actions of addicts. It's the same reason we don't stick our hands in fire, and we flush away our waste. Our bodies and our minds -- when we are healthy-minded -- reject that which is harmful to us.

Addiction mutes the voice of self-love. Addiction tells us that we deserve whatever horrible things happen to us in its service. And for many of us, that voice was silenced before we even knew there was some substance out there that would ease our pain. I recently read an essay by a woman who had to become the "woman of the house" at the age of seven. Her womanly duties included sexually pleasing her father. At the age of seven, she had no idea how to say to no to him. The pain of her early life drove her to relentlessly pursue perfection -- a goal she could never reach. She was able to hear the voice of self-preservation briefly, but something caused it to go silent again and she eventually committed suicide. We don't all get the happy ending.

For some life can be brutal. For others the problem is that life can be just too damn easy. When a parent arbitrarily says no or never says no, our own "no" muscle doesn't get a lot of exercise.

Some parents never expect their children do anything. They don't make them turn off the TV and read a book. They don't make them do chores or earn money. They don't push them to stick with a discipline of any kind. A man who worked all the time while his son was young now tries to make it up to him by giving him whatever he wants. He does his son's laundry, pays for his college even though the son doesn't go to classes, and gives the kid free rein with a credit card. As a college teacher, I come across young people who are astounded when they are told they actually have to do certain things in order to pass the class.

Sometimes the results can be disastrous. A family I know is now mourning the loss by suicide of a son who was never given boundaries. When this child acted out, he was placated time and again. He was never required or expected to respect his parents. He never developed the ability of restraint. In a fit of passion he shot himself.

My mother was also one who was not good at saying no to me; my "no" muscle was subsequently pretty weak. I said yes to everything -- unless it was too difficult or demanding. After years of making lousy choices, I had to turn within and ask for help in learning how to say "no." It has taken years of practice, but I now say no to all kinds of things that don't serve me well. I don't drink caffeine. I don't eat things that make me feel bad. I don't hang around negative people.

I have not only learned how to say "no"; I have also learned how to listen to the voice within when my emotions threaten to override my common sense. I recently wanted to quit my job. I was angry about the way the administration did something, and I was feeling stifled. Then that self-preservation voice in all its reasonableness spoke up. It reminded me of the things I love about my job. It reminded me of the students who bring so much pleasure to my life. It also reminded me that I am responsible for my situation. I decided not to quit. Instead I went back to work with more enthusiasm, determined to give more than I took. That was a wise choice, and I am grateful I listened.

My brother David tells a story in a similar vein about how he quit smoking. He was in his 20s and an actor at the time, and he had begun smoking for a role. He liked it and continued to smoke. A couple of years later he was doing a show on a cruise ship. He'd gone out on the deck to have a cigarette when a man, who was in his 60s but looked to be in his 70s, came out.

"It was an elegant ship with a long spiral staircase to the upper deck. When this man reached the top of the staircase, he was hacking and coughing for a good five minutes. As soon as his coughing fit ended, the man lit up a cigarette. I realized at that moment that everything I do now is a vote for or against my future self."

My brother crumpled up his pack of Marlboros and threw them away. He never smoked again. His realization was that inner wisdom, giving him a chance to change his fate.

Remember this: *every single action you make in this moment is a vote for or against your future self.*

Meditation

I've heard so many people say, "Oh, I can't meditate. I can't get my mind to stay still." Sorry, but I'm just going to be blunt here—that's a lame excuse. The other alibi people often use is that they don't have time to meditate.

Here's the deal—there isn't a list of rules for meditating. From what I understand, no one can get their mind to stay perfectly still. That's why the Buddhists call it "monkey mind." My brother, John, who is a great proponent of meditation, says that when he meditates, he merely watches his thoughts unravel. The idea is not to hold onto any thoughts. Let the thoughts flow in and flow out. Allow the stillness to come to you, don't force it. If the stillness doesn't come, don't worry. Simply allow yourself to be.

Some people say you should meditate at the same time every day in the same place for at least ten or twenty or thirty minutes. Many insist that you should meditate in the mornings before you start your day. But for me that doesn't work. I'm a morning person. When I get up, I love to jump into my work. However, what I will often do is sit down first thing with my journal and a cup of tea. I write down my dreams from the night before, anything interesting that has happened to me recently and what I intend to accomplish that day. I often write down an affirmative prayer or "spiritual mind treatment." I've noticed that on those days I'm usually more productive than on days when I don't do this. I think it helps me to get focused.

My meditation time comes in the afternoon usually, after I've gotten some work done. I may sit in my big comfortable chair in my room or on the porch.

Sometimes I say a mantra, perhaps a Sanskrit phrase if I'm feeling "Eastern" that day or often it may be something as simple as "thank you" or "I love you." You can imagine the cares of the day being lifted from your spirit in the form of smoke or steam.

Meditation is simply the time you make to be with yourself, to touch the stillness (or not), to breathe and to allow your unconscious mind a chance to commune with your conscious mind.

Breath is an important part of meditation, because slow easy breathing calms us and heals us. There are many breath-work teachings that can help you learn how to use the breath for spiritual development. One simple method is to breathe in slowly to the count of four, hold the breath for a few seconds and slowly exhale, completely emptying the lungs. Then begin again.

Another breathing method, frequently taught in yoga classes, is to breathe in one nostril while holding the other nostril closed. Then close the first nostril and release the other nostril and exhale. Then breathe in through the second nostril, close it and exhale out the first nostril.

The Buddhists recommend an attitude of mindfulness. Thich Nhat Hanh described the process to Oprah Winfrey this way: "Suppose you are drinking a cup of tea. When you hold your cup, you may like to breathe in, to bring your mind back to your body, and you become fully present. And when you are truly there, something else is also there—life, represented by the cup of tea. In that moment you are real, and the cup of tea is real. You are not lost in the past, in the future, in your projects, in your worries. You are free from all of these afflictions. And in that state of being free, you enjoy your tea. That is the moment of happiness, and of peace. When you brush your teeth, you may have just two minutes, but according to this practice, it is possible to produce freedom and joy during that time, because you are established in the here and now. If you are capable of brushing your teeth in mindfulness, then you will be able to enjoy the time when you take a shower, cook your breakfast, sip your tea."

If the word "meditation" seems too daunting, you can simply choose a word other than meditation to describe what you do as Tim McKee describes in his blog "This Very Second." He says that sometimes he'll simply rub my own heart in small circles and say, "Everything is OK, Tim" over and over.

Case Study, John: John, a musician and teacher in St. Louis, was a big drinker and a heavy partier. Eventually, he grew tired of this behavior. He joined A.A. and made a crucial discovery.

John: In A.A. I learned that your Higher Power could be anything you said it was. God could therefore be a group. So I visualized the AA group surrounding me. I turned over my desire to drink to them. This actually represented a whole different way of thinking for me. All my life I thought, I don't need anyone to do anything for me. I don't need help. That doesn't mean I was responsible. In my deepest inner self I believed I was all powerful and could do anything I wanted to do. The breakthrough came in asking for help, admitting I couldn't do it. I asked my friends in my mind to take this pitcher of beer, and when I did that, I let go. That was the first time I had ever let go, and I felt this euphoria at saying "I can't handle it" and really meaning it. Prior to that, I always said, "Show me the trick or give me the instructions, and I can do anything." I had never admitted that I couldn't do something.

This was radically different, and I had this euphoric experience. I sat there in that euphoria for about a minute. Wow, I just let go. The second part of the A.A. third step is "came to believe a power greater than ourselves could restore us to sanity." At first I thought that the power greater than myself was the group. I turned my will over to the group. Then that euphoric experience itself turned into the divine awareness. After the euphoria, I felt a tremendous calm and warmth—a vast, infinite experience.

I realized 'This is God.' I was driving in my truck, and had a gigantic awareness that I was now experiencing God. The other thing had just been a doorway. God showed me this vast unity and peace and harmony. I was amazed at everything. It was way beyond a drug experience. I was completely conscious, completely in control, totally aware. I pulled up in front of my house, turned off the motor, and the experience went away.

The next morning I went to my AA meeting and told what had happened, and the experience came back. I went to nine meetings that day. Every time I told it, it came back. The bottom line is that I realized there is a God and God is different for everybody. My God was not a guy with a beard. My God was a feeling about everything, an awareness that everything was connected to me and that any time I focused on it, that energy would be working for me. It is flowing in my direction all the time. Sometimes I anthropomorphize it, I make it into a personality I can talk to, but most of the time God is everything working together, flowing— divine consciousness.

Make it work for you:

1. Write your own prayer. Write it in the present tense. Begin with gratitude. End with praise.

   Example:

   Thank you, Divine Intelligence, for the freedom to choose my good. I am open and receptive to the energy of love flowing through the Universe. Thank you for erasing my fear and easing my pain. I now experience the love of God every moment of every day. I am beautiful. I am beloved. I am a magnificent expression of the great creative power of God.

   Note: you do not have to use the word "God." You don't even have to believe in "God." You simply have to believe that something inside you wants the very best for you. Appeal to that part of your interior self.

2. Spend some time in nature. Go to a park by yourself, walk and observe everything around you. Spend twenty minutes without speaking, pay attention to your breath, pay attention to the sounds outside and the sounds inside. Stop, look around, be present.

THREE
Change Your Self-Image

When I was in high school, I began smoking cigarettes. I didn't like them much, but they fit my image of the cool rebel-girl I thought that I was. One of my good friends was a boy we called Spock because he was thin and pale and looked like a Vulcan. Spock did not smoke and he didn't like it that I did. One day as we were sitting outside school, I lit up a cigarette, and he asked me why I smoked.

"I just picture myself with a cigarette in my hand," I told him.

"Why can't you picture yourself eating an apple instead?" he asked. How utterly logical.

I eventually quit smoking. I'm not sure if I used Spock's advice, but I never forgot it. Years later when addictions of a different sort were ruining my life, I had to recall that simple little piece of advice and replace one self-image with another.

This, I believe, is one of the fundamental keys to eliminating addiction. Whatever our addiction is, it has become integrally woven with our self-image. For many addicts, that image is one of victimization. We're victims of one thing or another—bad parents, abusive spouses, lousy schools, or our own uncontrollable impulses. A woman I know wanted to write a screenplay—a satire, she said, detailing the way certain unkind folks in the film industry had treated her.

"Let it go," I told her. "You can't spend the rest of your life being a victim."

Victims tend to make excuses. They blame others for their situations. This is not to suggest that bad things don't happen to us. They do. The question is, how do you perceive yourself, day in and day out? How do you present yourself to the world? As a victim or a victor?

My friend Samantha had bone cancer when she was a teenager. Her leg was amputated just above the thigh and she wore a prosthesis that she jokingly called her "Barbie leg." Samantha had every reason in the world to feel victimized, and I'm sure there were times when she wondered, why me? But she didn't turn her life into a pity party. Instead she focused on all the love in her life, and she created even more. She was the first one to volunteer to come help with a birthday party. She loved to garden and knew the name of just about every kind of flower in existence. Whenever there was a challenge, Samantha wanted to face it. She hiked, camped and swam. She didn't always wear her prosthesis, and she didn't care what other people thought of her. She would practice her Tai Chi in the lobby of a movie theater if she felt like it.

Seventeen years after her first bout with cancer, Sam was diagnosed with breast cancer. During the last few months of her life, she was in terrible pain, and yet she never lacked for friends, friends who wanted to help her out not because they were such altruistic people but because it was great fun to be with her. With her warm smile and her kindness, she made it a joy to be around her even as she was dying. Samantha is one of my heroes. I remember her whenever I begin to feel sorry for myself about some minor disruption in my life. It's a truism, but one that can make an enormous difference in life: You can't always control the circumstances of your life, but you can control how you react to them.

Change Your Mind

There's a song that was constantly on the radio a while back. The words were: If you want to change your life, change your mind. But in order to change your mind, it helps to be totally clear about what you want.

Junkies can manifest drugs, money, and drama like Jesus turning water into wine. The reason for this is that addicts are absolutely clear. They wake up every single morning, and they know exactly what it is that they want. There's no distraction—there's no attention on what they don't want. They are totally clear. Until one day a little bit of ambivalence creeps in. They might look around and think to themselves, wait a minute, this isn't really fun anymore. Other people are happier than I am. Other people don't feel like crap all the time. Other people are having fun, and I'm working all the time; being an addict is a 24-7 job. As soon as the ambivalence creeps in, then the picture shifts. There's room for a new idea to enter.

What are the images you carry about in your head? Deborah, one of the case studies in this book, said that she used to have images of self-destruction pop up in her mind: stabbing herself, shooting herself, injuring herself in one fashion or another. She said she didn't do those things, but the pictures came to her mind involuntarily. It wasn't a conscious act. She had to learn to immediately replace those images with something else—for instance, a mental picture of herself laughing with friends, walking along the beach, climbing a mountain, or delivering a speech. The self-destructive images continued to enter her mind unbidden for a long time, but she didn't let them linger. She didn't give them free rent in her head.

Author Wayne Dyer says "If you can see it, you can believe it." He means that if you can create a picture in your mind of what you want, you can eventually manifest that picture in reality. This is the whole concept of visualization. Many times people use visualization to acquire things. They might cut out pictures of the car they want or the kind of house they'd like to live in and post them in a visible place. But you don't have to limit this technique to things. You can create images of the kind of person you would like to be and these images will slowly (or sometimes immediately) begin to replace the old pictures of who you think you are. It's very difficult for us to give up our identity—even if that identity is as a drunk, a thief or a worthless loser. But if there's something better to replace it, we can gradually accept a new persona—a new idea of ourselves. Inside we're always the same. We are Spirit, beautiful, loving and joy filled. So it's not like we're changing some essential part of our nature. It's more like putting on new clothes.

In *A Course in Miracles*, the idea of the Law of the Kingdom is explained this way: "When a brother perceives himself as sick, he is perceiving himself as not whole, and therefore in need. If you, too, see him this way, you are seeing him as if he were absent from the Kingdom or separated from it, thus making the Kingdom itself obscure to both of you."

When I was in my full blown druggie consciousness, I saw myself as an outlaw with nothing to lose. My mother, on the other hand, kept a different image alive for me. She knew how to see the Truth. The whole time that I was doggedly trying to destroy myself, my mother refused to see anything but my absolute perfection. And she told me this. She said I know who you are. This is not who you are. This is an illusion. And she was right.

And so eventually my picture shifted, and my reality changed. I created a new reality. I saw myself as a college girl, and I became a college girl. A few years later I graduated magna cum laude. Then, I guess I got stuck in that image, because I went on to get two more degrees. But that was a better place to be stuck than where I had been before.

Author and spiritual teacher Deepak Chopra writes in *The Seven Spiritual Laws of Success* that we bring about change by two qualities which are inherent in consciousness: attention and intention. "Attention energizes, and intention transforms." If you put your attention on some aspect of your life, that aspect will grow. Have you ever noticed how obsessive addicts are? They put all their attention on the object of their affection. And so that object becomes the most important thing in their lives. However, if you take your attention away from something, it will wither away and die.

So you begin with an intention. For instance, "I intend to stop drinking." Now, what do you intend to do instead? "I intend to spend more time with my family." The intention, as Chopra writes, "triggers transformation of energy and information." You have made your intention known to the universe. Now, you must pull your attention away from drinking and place it on your family.

As a result of my fondness for needles in the 1970s, I was infected with hepatitis C. I lived with the disease for many years, before it started to affect my life. When I was finally diagnosed, I didn't want to get the treatment because it was expensive, took many months to complete, and was not always effective. I thought I could manage without it. But after a couple of years of battling the fatigue, the memory loss and other unpleasant symptoms of the disease, I began to see myself as a sick person. I didn't like to make plans because I never knew how I was going to feel on any given day. Eventually, that got old, and I became determined to see myself as a well person instead of someone who lived in bed. My intention became clear: get healthy. So I found a good doctor, got a liver biopsy and started taking the Interferon-Ribivirin treatment. The doctor warned me that the treatment had severe side effects, one of which was supposed to be depression. Well, I did experience most of those side effects. I felt fatigued. I lost a lot of my hair. I had very little energy, and my immune system was definitely a 90-pound weakling. But never, not even once, did I get depressed. I was so clear. I wanted my health back, and every shot of Interferon and every Ribivirin pill that I took brought me closer to health. Even when I was feeling really crummy, I would say to myself, "I am healthy. I am healthy." I kept my attention on the end result, and I had faith—faith in my doctor, faith in my body and faith that Spirit was responding to my belief. Six months passed. I no longer had to take the medication, and the blood results came back—negative for hepatitis C. I am healthy.

In *The Four Agreements*, Don Miguel Ruiz, tells us to "be impeccable" with our word. This is the foundation for many of the "new thought" religions, and it is also the idea behind affirmations. Your words are extremely powerful. I overcame my drug addiction many years ago, but that doesn't mean my life suddenly became problem-free as I expected it would. As I joined the middle class and had more mainstream aspirations, I also had to deal with finances, and I wasn't very good at it. I tended to worry a lot about how to pay for this thing or that, and I talked about it constantly. I saw myself as poor and others began to reinforce that view because I wouldn't let them think of me as any other way. I would complain, I would make statements such as "I'm broke," and I would get into a competitive "poor me" match with anyone who was willing. Interestingly enough, none of those things were effective in making me richer or alleviating my financial difficulties.

Learning to be careful of the words I said was one of the hardest things I've ever done. I have so many choices of words to put behind "I am." Even when it does appear to me that I am having financial problems, it is important for me to know it is a temporary condition and not to get locked into an identity of "I am broke." Delete that. I am rich.

In his book, *Power Through Constructive Thinking*, Emmet Fox offers a wonderful prescription for detoxifying your mind. It's called the "Seven Day Mental Diet." As Fox explains, the thoughts that you think and the subjects you allow your mind to dwell upon make you and your surroundings what they are. "Thought is the real causative force in your life and there is no other."

In order to begin the process of changing your thinking, Fox says that for seven days you should not allow yourself to dwell for a single moment on any kind of negative thought. That means no complaining, no whining, no grousing. You can start at any time, but it is wise to prepare yourself for a day or two. You might want to write down some affirmations, such as "My life is good," "Everything is for me, nothing is against me," "I am in charge of my own mind." Now, I can tell you from personal experience that this diet is not easy. And Fox says that if you mess up, then you need to start the seven days all over again. But once you get in the habit of paying attention to your thoughts, you really can change your life. And you will certainly change your attitude about life. We'll discuss the idea of the mental diet further in Chapter 5.

There is a trick to all this, you know. Of course, you already figured that. The trick is gratitude. Be grateful. Be grateful for the possibilities. Be grateful that you have the potential to be whatever it is your heart desires. Be grateful for freedom from your addictions and know in your heart that you are free. Allow yourself to feel that freedom. It is yours. All you have to do is accept it.

Tess Marshall, a substance abuse counselor and spiritual workshop leader, describes her transition from smoker to health nut in her book *Flying by the Seat of the Soul*. Tess explains that she started smoking as a teenager, but when she became a mother she hid her smoking from her children so they wouldn't follow her example. Finally, she knew she couldn't hide it anymore. She had to quit. She writes, "I knew that in order to be successful I had to replace smoking with something else. . . . I began running on an indoor track at the local college. When I began, I walked more than I ran. I added a lap every week; my goal was to add an additional mile every month. The following spring on a sunny spring day in April I ran outside for the first time. I was up to five miles! I began running in the evenings, one hour after our family finished eating dinner together. I would lace up my shoes and hit the road feeling very free. It became my alone time and Roger's time with the children. Strength and courage allowed me to take control of my life. Running gave me time to clear my head, it kept me sane."

From Convict to Celebrity Chef

You may have heard of Chef Jeff Henderson, the celebrated author and star of a reality TV show. Chef Jeff learned how to cook in prison. I heard him at a speaking engagement describe how he had to learn how to smile at people, how to dress, how to comport himself like a chef instead of a convict. He changed his inner image and his outer image. It must have worked because look at him now!

Case Study, Lorri: Lorri and I met by happenstance. She was the friend of a friend, and she was in trouble. She'd lost her job and needed somewhere to stay. I was recently separated from my husband and had plenty of room in my house. I didn't know at first that she was dealing with a severe addiction problem, but I knew something wasn't right with her health, and I suspected that the cure lay within her. We spoke a lot about how to create lasting change. Things didn't get better overnight for Lorri, but I have witnessed remarkable changes in her over the past year and a half.

Lorri: I walk down a dark alley way, sleeves rolled up anticipating an ambient rush in the night. Arms bruised and battered from the night before, but that day is over and the feeling is gone. Doubled over in pain, looking for some sweet juice to lighten up the way but it is all gone. It's over. The only light I see now is the one on the ambulance. No one else is coming; no one else is left. The door is closed tight. No one has the key, except the patrolman in blue, gun by his side, cuffs clanging behind him waiting for my pale thin arms. Seriously, it's over! The smell of sweat and vomit encompasses the vacant room as tears soak through my dirty t-shirt. Sirens ring in the background as I stumble over the last step. The sun fell hours ago. Only the desperate are out tonight. Whispering my name, in a shaky voice to the lady in the fresh white scrubs. "Come with me," she says, walking down the newly painted corridor, "we have one room left."

A hospital gown and a bed lay before me. But what I needed most was a shower to wash away the night before. A haggard old nurse walked beside me with a drawer filled with Phenobarbital, Librium, and Seboxone to help with the shaking and the opiate withdrawal. The nurse gave me a Librium to hold me over till the blood results came in. Sixteen hours later, I woke up to the sun blazing in my bloodshot eyes and a tray of heat-up food in front of me. I scarfed it down like it was the last meal on earth. It must have been 72 hours since my last meal; anything tasted good at this point. I stood up and made my way to the shower. Hot steamy water streaming down on my aching head, I took the small bar of soap and cradled it in my hand massaging every inch of my smell ridden body. My other hand held the rails as I propped my limp body up straight.

Twenty minutes later I staggered to the kitchen and raided the refrigerator; vanilla ice cream is easy on the stomach. I noticed three other people leaning on the table, nuzzled in their seats staring at the midday news. I wondered what their poison is. None of them looked much healthier than me, except they were sitting in an upright position. That's progress I thought. I strolled on back to bed, lay my head down and wondered how it ever got this bad.

It started two and half years ago, when a knee injury sent me to the Emergency Room where I was given a prescription for Vicodin and a shot of Demerol for instant relief. A euphoric feeling crept over me, and the pain was gone. Knee surgery led to more Vicodin and Percocet, which eventually played havoc with my stomach. One day, doubled over in pain, I decided to go to the Emergency Room again, this time for my stomach. They gave me an injection of Dilaudid, a day that changed my life. A once in a lifetime visit became a weekly routine. Two milligrams of Dilaudid every four hours is what the doctor ordered-inpatient! Sweet Jesus, could it get any better than that? The doctors ran every test known to man and everything came up negative. Healthy, even the chest x-rays showed me to be a non-smoker, which was not true.

On the weeks I was discharged, I would take the Vicodin and Percocet provided to me by pain management for my torn ACL, and daily visits to the ER for injections of Dilaudid for my stomach. Sometimes they would admit me for three to four days and I would get the Dilaudid every four hours on the buzzer exactly to the minute. It's legal though, I thought, nurses are shooting me up with prescribed medications, it can't be wrong. The pain was real and at this point it didn't matter. I was a legal junkie, slowly withering away.

I suffered blackouts from the Dilaudid, but the instant rush kept me alive. Deathly ill on the days I didn't go to the hospital. Barely making it through the day, six Percocets to make it tolerable and four Vicodins to top it off. Ambulance rides in the middle of the night. Twenty inpatient stays since January and countless ER visits just to get a fix. Addicted!

I don't know when I crossed the line, but I know I crossed into the darkness early on. I couldn't stop. The feeling of life (or is it death) creeping through my veins, the liquid drug crawling through every fiber of my being. From the moment the needle touched the port, I could feel the journey radiate through my body. No words can explain it. No feeling can replace it. It made me feel so alive and healthy, yet it killed my spiritual life, my emotional life. Friends turned their backs on me. No one even visited me when I went to the hospital anymore and I'd put a dagger through my family ties. The end! I had reached the end. I was all alone in a world of sickness and disease.

When I got out of the hospital, my sister dumped me at my friend Pat's house. I was pretty sure Pat didn't want me back. I had vomited on the carpet, and police had come by the house twice. Not only that, my best friend and former sponsor would have nothing more to do with me.

"No ambulances, no police, or you're out of here," Pat told me. I had nowhere else to go. I realized I had two choices: kill myself or change something. Something inside me decided I wasn't ready to die yet. I set an intention to change.

Three months later, I sit in a Starbucks sipping on some raspberry tea, a million thoughts strutting across my mind. My health has been mostly stable and I found a new home for fellowship and friendship. A new AA group has taken a liking to me and I accept it slowly yet gratefully. I let bits and pieces get out about my desperate times with Dilaudid and how bad it had gotten. They give me a hug and a smile and welcome me anyway. I feel accepted without putting up a front. I can be myself, whoever that might be. My image of myself has changed. I'm not an addict. Instead I'm a web designer; I'm a writer; I'm a college student. Sometimes I feel lost and broken, yet other times I know I can hold it all together.

When I was a child I never dreamed my life would turn out this way. I had always been leery of drugs and alcohol, aware of the results from using substances to alter your mind's thinking. However, as I got older the need to escape became far greater than the need to feel. I found that if I was high I could fit in to a world I didn't feel a part of.

Today, I must learn to feel a part of the world I'm so uncomfortable in without the use of alcohol and drugs. Surrounding myself with sober people and going to 12-step meetings seem to be the only answer. I am learning to love and care for people in a way I was incapable of doing just months ago. I have many fears and challenges ahead. Yet I will be able to get through them. I must learn to reach out to other sober people instead of isolating myself. I must stand tall and not let my pride get in the way of my progress.

Everything I lost -- my home, my job, my friends, my family -- are slowly coming back to me a day at a time. I am a full time student now, working to better my life. The God thing will be icing on the cake if it's true. I am still an agnostic but am keeping an open mind. Pat says that the "something inside me" is my god-self. That's a hard concept for me, but as I practice mindfulness meditation, I find the strength to do the next right thing. And that is really all that anyone can do, with or without a god. Be good, love one another, and do the next right thing.

Make it work for you:

1. Make a treasure book. First step is to buy a photo album. Then get magazines, catalogs and a pair of scissors and start cutting. Would you like to dress with a little more style? Put pictures of nice clothes on your pages. Do you want to be healthier? Put in pictures of people engaged in healthy activities—jogging, swimming, having fun. I put pictures of women doing yoga in my treasure book, and soon a yoga class was offered at the Y nearby. I've been going twice a week ever since, and I can almost do the poses in my treasure book. Be sure to include symbols that resonate for you on a spiritual level—nature scenes or words such as "Joy." Write out a blue sky list—a list of things you'd like to accomplish or ways you'd like to see yourself. Write it in the first person present tense, i.e. "I am at my ideal weight." You can put your blue sky list in your treasure book or somewhere else you can see it often. Look at your book often. Notice what begins to manifest in your life.

2. In addition to visualization, use your words to change your self-image. Make everything you say an affirmation of something positive or desirable. Avoid gossip. Try to find something good to say about other people. If you find your conversations revolve around how rotten everything is, keep a few "conversation detours" handy. For instance, a good movie you've seen or a good book you've read or a recipe that you've tried recently. Write a list of the good things in your life every day so they'll be fresh in your mind when you need something to talk about with other people.

3. Who are your heroes? Are they complainers or whiners?
    Probably not. Write down their good qualities. Now, imagine that
    those same qualities belong to you. Act as if and you will be as if.

FOUR
Get a Little Help From Your Friends

"When we gather to create the spiritual consciousness we help each other more than can be described. We are social creatures. Society has its own messages that it conveys to us about greed, anger, resentment, fear and so on. So we need each other, spiritually, to come together in whatever way we can in order to share the spiritual view, cleanse, and work with ourselves and each other."

--John MacEnulty
Eman8tions, "Thought For the Day"

"I'm just not a joiner," a woman told me. She was one of the most friendless and unhappy people I ever knew. I couldn't understand why she would want to continue to live like that.

You don't have to be a "joiner" to become a member of a spiritual community. In fact, you may not have much in common with the other people who belong to the spiritual community of your choice. You go there to get a dose of love and positive feedback. Joining a church or other spiritual community doesn't mean you have to make it your life, but it can provide a great way to meet friends and network with people who are willing to support you in a number of ways.

What is a spiritual community? Well, it can be a church, but doesn't have to be. I personally have sought out a church that does not espouse blame or judgment. I've had enough of that. Unity, Religious Science, Unitarian churches, Buddhist or Hindu temples, synagogues, the local YMCA all provide meeting places for positive people. In addition to religious gatherings, you may find your spiritual community in a yoga or tai chi class, or an ethical humanist group. There are groups that meet to discuss *A Course in Miracles* or some other spiritual text. You may find that your AA or NA group provides that sense of spiritual community. If you are looking for enlightenment, you might even find a guru who can help you.

Twelve-step programs are wonderful. I've known many people whose lives have been saved by them. And there are 12-step programs for nearly every addictive disorder. These programs work because they have a spiritual foundation, and because of the one-on-one support of a sponsor. In addition, the people in your group have been where you have been and won't judge you. Colin is one of those people who credits AA with helping him overcome a twenty-year battle with drugs and alcohol. But it didn't happen overnight. The first time he joined AA he sobered up for three months. He backslid and found himself drunk again, so drunk that he was beaten up by police and arrested. Fortunately, he was accepted into a treatment program to detox. After three weeks he left the treatment program and began to return to AA meetings. The next time he was sober for a year. Once again he had a relapse into his alcoholism. After another bout with drugs and alcohol, he found himself listening to a drunken friend.

"It was like looking into the mirror," he said. "This guy was saying the same old tired lies I had been telling myself for years."

Colin eventually found the power and strength to get sober and stay sober through AA. He later began to explore spirituality in depth. We'll reveal more of his story in a later chapter.

Not everyone responds to the 12-step program structure. If you are one of those, then you should actively search for some other form of spiritual sustenance. I don't believe that real recovery is possible without some kind of spiritual support.

Churches and other spiritual communities give you a chance to be someone you might not have been before. They provide a great place to get a hug, a smile, a cup of coffee. You might say, how hypocritical, what do any of these things have to do with God? Everything. God is in every good hug, in every smile and even in that cup of coffee that someone made for you.

If you wind up in a church that expects you to go out and proselytize or wants to know your activities and whereabouts all the time, then you should seek out a different place. You don't need another mother or father. You need spiritual brothers and sisters.

The best thing to do is to try a few different places. Where do you feel most at home? When my daughter was three years old, I decided it was time for me to find a church. I hadn't regularly attended since I was about 12, but I wanted my child to grow up with a spiritual foundation. I went to one church with a friend of mine. Everyone was all dressed up. The minister's sermon that day was on why "God" is a he. And no one stopped to smile at me. I decided not to go back. A few weeks later on a Sunday morning I was reading the Saturday paper which had the religion section. A local Unity minister had a column in it. The minister was a woman with short spiky hair, and her column was about a loving, nonjudgmental God. I called the church right then and asked if you had to get dressed up to go. "No, lots of people wear jeans," the lady on the phone said.

So I threw on a pair of jeans, took my child and immediately found a church home.

Now, because churches are full of people, I haven't encountered one yet that didn't have political fighting and other nonsense associated with it. But I continue to go anyway because I know at least once a week I'm going to walk into a place where everyone smiles at me, I get a lot of hugs and I get to sing some uplifting music even though my singing voice is less than wonderful. If I don't feel like socializing afterwards, I don't have to. I can go, get my heart recharged and come back home. But if I'm troubled, then I know I can turn to someone and get some prayer work—no questions asked.

The truth is that your spiritual community may simply consist of two or three people who are willing to know the highest and best for you. Even if you are not a "joiner," there is a way for you to surround yourself with like-minded people. Just keep looking until you find it.

Case Study, Nancy: Nancy is a former crack cocaine user. She is one of those who tried the 12-step programs but found that she wasn't comfortable in them. Fortunately, she found another place for spiritual development.

Nancy: I was looking for a way to get out of the insanity. It was taking a toll on me. Even though I was drinking and doing drugs, I was depressed inside. I knew I would never experience a greater life if I continued to live this way. I remember once I was sitting at a table and had all this crack in front of me, and I just felt so unhappy. It wasn't fun anymore. I didn't know anybody to hang around with that wasn't using something. That's all I ever knew. I can remember thinking, no decent guy is going to want me. My relationships were abusive, I had lost my job, and it had gotten to the point I was going to lose my family.

My sister was in religious science, so I decided to give it a try. I went to the Center for Positive Living, a new thought church. First they gave me a way to deal with my problems. But they also told me, "You are at choice." And I felt comfortable because I didn't need to identify myself as an alcoholic or an addict. The spirituality resonated really good with me. Now, I have a place to go where no one judges me and friends who are positive and supportive.

Make it work for you:

Look in the religion section of your local newspaper or under churches in your telephone book, circle three or four places that look interesting to you. Try a different one each week. Did any of those places make you feel at home? Was there a nonjudgmental atmosphere? If you can't find a religious community that suits you, perhaps you can try a yoga or tai chi class. There may be an ethical humanist group that meets for discussions. Ask your inner spirit for guidance to your right and perfect spiritual home.

FIVE
Change Your Mental Diet

"We become like the music we listen to, the literature we read, the programs we watch, the thoughts we think, and the companions we choose."

-- William Arthur Ward

We are bombarded with negativity on a daily basis. People at work gossip. Our family or friends complain. The television and newspapers feed on stories about serial killers, wars and natural disasters. When we get too much of this negative energy whirling around us, we wind up in "judgment mode." You know what I mean—pointing accusing fingers at this or that group of people or this or that individual. Our egos suck that stuff down like cotton candy. For instance if I read in the paper about an abusive parent, I can swell up my chest, look down my nose and say what a great parent I am because I would never treat a child that way.

I know someone who is a "news junkie." His eyes are glued to the television set for every "news event" from latest celebrity scandal to the latest military strike. He gets to be prosecutor, judge and jury all wrapped up in one unhappy package. He feels superior to all sorts of people, but his life revolves around these manufactured dramas rather than around the love and joy that is always available to all of us.

The tricky thing about judgment mode is that although it seems to be making us feel good about ourselves, it inevitably turns against us. We're so busy finding flaws in others that the critic within eventually starts noticing our own flaws and then we're in real trouble. That self-criticism can lead us right into the vortex. We begin to feel a sense of self-loathing as we tally up our imperfections. So we do something to numb that feeling which makes us loathe ourselves more.

The Sufi poet Rumi says, "Out beyond ideas of wrongdoing and rightdoing, there is a field. I'll meet you there."

There are times when you need to turn off the television, read the comics and throw the rest of the paper in the recycling bin, and avoid the gossipers and complainers in your life. Cultivate a friend or a prayer partner with whom you can share your blessings. Draw to you that one person who says, "Things are great" when you ask her how she's doing. When people ask how you are, do as one of my friends does: smile and say "Beautiful."

Okay, but the truth may be that you're feeling lousy. Maybe you're angry, broke, just got dumped and what you really want to do is get a drink or a shot or a double cheeseburger with extra-large fries or whatever it is you do when you're miserable. This is when a spiritual community comes in handy because what you need at this time is not to be around people who will feel sorry for you, look down upon you or out-do you in misery. Rather, these are the times when you need people who will remind you of how wonderful you are and how wonderful life is.

Fortunately, even if no one else is available, you can always do this for yourself. Sit down and write all the things you have to be grateful for. Maybe you can't think of any at first, but start with the simple things— lungs to breathe air, hands, feet, arms, whatever you have. Then you can look around—is it raining, be grateful you aren't in a drought. Is the sun shining? Open your eyes to the beauty around you. Eventually things are going to get better. You just have to stick around.

One of the best ways to break free from the vortex of negative energy is to read spiritual books. When I'm feeling desperate, frightened or worried, I often read the Psalms. It's a good idea to read something spiritual every day though admittedly we don't all do it. Alan Cohen sends out a "Daily Inspiration" on the Internet. It's usually a gentle spiritual reminder to meditate, to love or to embrace humility. Even if I've forgotten to pray or meditate that day, that little message is a reminder of the divinity that is always within me.

When I was about 18 years old, I read the novel *Siddhartha* by Herman Hesse. I still have a tattered paperback copy on my shelf. In the story a young man named Siddhartha leaves his family to become a contemplative. But he becomes bored with the religious life and embarks upon a path of lust and greed. Eventually, this dissolute life leads him to the brink of despair. He runs away and comes to a river where he meets a holy man. The holy man urges him to listen to the voice of the river. As he does so, Siddhartha ceases fighting his destiny.

"There shone in his face the serenity of knowledge, of one who is no longer confronted with conflict of desires, who has found salvation, who is in harmony with the stream of events, with the stream of life, full of sympathy and compassion, surrendering himself to the stream, belonging to the unity of all things."

I spent several years after reading this book following my own path of lust, greed and dissolution. And yet the ideas in that book haunted me. This notion of unity and peace had become imprinted on my mind. I knew there was something better than drugs and the destructive path I had chosen. I believed that if Siddhartha could find it, I could find it as well. It didn't matter that the book was a work of fiction. There was a truth inside that story which resonated in my soul.

Case Study, Stephanie: Stephanie is not a former addict or alcoholic but she was married to an alcoholic and that led her to Al-anon. For many years she was an agnostic—painfully so. The story of how she found herself on a spiritual path is one that I love:

I was raised in a traditional Christian church, but I stopped believing in God or anything metaphysical in college. I saw all the troubles that religion had caused, and I could see no scientific basis for any belief in the supernatural. But then as I got older I was deeply unhappy. I was married to an alcoholic for years before I finally realized I had to do something. Now, I never would have gone to any organization that had anything to do with the word "God." But they didn't talk about God—they just mentioned that "higher power" business. So that is how my mind finally opened up a little. Then shortly before my mother died, I witnessed some things that just weren't possible. She had Alzheimer's and was

*physically debilitated. Well, a few days before she died, she sat up—
which was physically impossible—and was completely lucid. And she
mentioned that she had seen my father and was going to go join him.
Then she died. When I saw that, it occurred to me that there was
something about people I didn't understand. But I didn't know how to find
out more. I just didn't think I'd find it in a traditional church.*

*One day I got something in the mail advertising "Science of Mind
Magazine." You could get one free trial issue and then cancel the
subscription if you didn't like it. Well, I thought I'd go ahead and look at
the magazine. I was pretty sure I would cancel it after the first issue.
When the first issue came, I didn't even read it. But I also forgot to cancel
the subscription. Then the next one came, and I thought, "Oh, now I'm
stuck with it." I opened up the magazine and started reading and didn't
put it down until I had read the whole thing. Then I went and found the
first one and read it. That led me to the foundational book, which I didn't
realize I already had on my own bookshelves, but had never read. Soon
after that I found a science of mind center, and I've been on a spiritual
path ever since.*

Make it work for you:

Go to the library, visit your church bookstore, look and see what's on your shelf that you haven't read before. Ask your friends what inspirational books they've read. If you're not a big reader, then get audio books. It's a wonderful way to pass time in the car.

The key word in this step is "change." Change something. Food addiction is as powerful as heroin addiction. Actually it's a worse addiction because you can give up heroin, but you can never completely give up food. So you must change something. An outer change will help to bring on an inner change. Change one thing a week. It doesn't have to be a big change. It can be a small change. Add a walk to your daily routine. Become a weekday vegetarian as Graham Hill advocates on *TEDTalks*.

Little changes will add up to big changes.

SIX
Express Your Divinity

In 1995, fifteen years after I had been incarcerated for drug-related offenses, I went back to prison—this time to teach creative writing. Thus began an important lesson for me in the curative power of the expressive arts. Over the next few years I taught poetry classes, drama workshops and other arts classes to numerous groups from juveniles in a court-ordered housing facility to jails to prisons to seminars for mental health professionals and chaplains to corporate employees to middle-school kids at a private school.

I discovered that the arts—poetry, dance, drawing, journaling, acting, music-making and so forth—are tools that anyone can use to express their divine creativity. In our society we have the strange idea that only the "highly talented" are entitled to these treasures. We think that you must go to specialized schools and earn degrees and be recognized by certain august organizations in order to be an artist. Everyone else is consigned to the role of audience or spectator. But other cultures know this isn't so. The arts are for everyone—not just to watch, admire and appreciate—but to do.

The arts serve many purposes which I will delineate further in this chapter. They can serve as a punching bag when we're angry, they can help us develop an identity more in keeping with our personal integrity, and they can help us express love.

So many people are so focused on their problems. Their entire attention is placed on their problems, so what does that create? More problems. Wherever your attention is placed that is what will show up in your life. This is why healthy people have hobbies. The arts give people a chance to think about something besides their problems.

We communicate with other people daily. We dispense information, ask questions, trade "small" talk and convey a variety of thoughts and ideas. But when it comes to talking about deeper feelings, fears, or concerns, we usually find we are at a loss for words. We find it difficult, if not impossible, to articulate the things that matter most to us. In addition, quite often we have information, which is vital to our emotional, physical or spiritual health, locked inside us somewhere. Unfortunately, we don't know how to access that information.

How can the arts help? Visual art, poetry, and dance use the language of the subconscious mind, the same language that our dreams use, the language of symbol and metaphor, to communicate with our conscious minds. Poet Chase Twichell says that poetry is a recording of "a mind communicating to others the experience of its own consciousness." Other artists will tell you that their art is how they discover what they think or how they feel about something. The arts provide a way for our deeper feelings to be expressed to us and to others. And unlike some other means that the subconscious may use, the arts are a healthy and safe form of expression. Many people do not realize that repressed emotions can have serious consequences, including miscommunication and misunderstanding, loss of self-esteem, and even illness -- not to mention addiction.

In order for any endeavor involving more than one person to succeed, those involved need clear and open channels of communication. They need to be able to be honest with each other. Each person should have a clear idea of their own thoughts and feelings so that they can communicate them. They also need to be able to see each other as fellow humans. If you only know a person's thoughts, then that person is little more than a machine, but if you know her feelings, then she becomes someone you can understand, relate to, and identify with. The arts help us connect as human beings.

My brother, John MacEnulty, wrote this as part of his daily "Thought for the Day" that he sends out to internet subscribers. It's a good description of the link between poetry and spirit (reprinted with permission from John MacEnulty):

There is poetry within us. When we nurture it, it grows, becomes our way of seeing, expressing.

I validate the beauty within, honor it as the best part of myself, practice releasing it, freeing it to speak to me, show me.

Poetry is the implication, the way the world speaks. It is the mystery whispered in my ear as I watch, listen, feel. It is the idea that flows in everything.

And everything contains a thought. And the divine is that thought.

It isn't necessarily religious or scriptural, this spiritual reality within all things. It is the essential joy of fascination.

It isn't how we act. It's how we feel. The energy that flows from that creates the thought, allows the beauty to emerge.

Poetry is the prayer of the creative mind, beauty, the love expressed to and through us.

It is the mystery within. The impossibility of understanding surrounds, fills our words, our thoughts, the mystery of wanting to touch but not touching, of wanting to sing but keeping our breath-filled silence. It is the fulfillment that dares not move, the magic we don't wish to understand, the invisible connection our stillness breathes and feels, then the words that do not break the silence but deepen it.

Case Study, Jimmy: Jimmy is a singer/songwriter, who lives in North Carolina. Part of the mythology of the music business is that drinking and drugging are part and parcel of "the life." Jimmy would disagree.

Jimmy: I got my first guitar when I was twelve years old. Music was always part of my life. At some point, drugs and alcohol also became part of my life. My drug of choice was "more." I couldn't just have one beer. I would drink till I dropped. Some nights after a show, I would go over to this cocaine dealer's house. We'd sit around playing guitars, drinking Heinekens and Jack Daniels and snorting lines until the sun rose. I'll always remember the way my friend would say, "Well, Jimmy, looks like the Big Eye caught us again."

Then on May 25, 1985, I went to my friend Bobby's house in Maryland for a crab feast. They had buckets of crabs and a keg of beer. We ate crabs and drank until about 7 or 7:30 and then went to a bar with a friend named Wendy to hear a band that I knew play. We got there and drank more beer and then we drank even more beer. Finally, at around 2 when the bar had to close, my friend in the band said, "You're not driving, are you?"

I said, "I have to. It's my car. Bobby's puking, and Wendy's passed out." My friend talked me into staying and having a cup of coffee with him. After about an hour, we left. We were in Maryland going to Virginia. Somewhere on the beltway my vision started getting blurry. I was terrified. I kept smacking Bobby and telling him that he had to be my eyes because I couldn't see.

Somehow we got home safely, and I had the sense not to try to leave. I stayed on his couch. But I couldn't sleep. I was just lying on that couch staring up at the ceiling. I was still consumed with fear, and I began to cry. I think I actually prayed to the ceiling. I said, "Oh, God, I don't ever want to be this scared again. Please take this away from me."

I've never had a drink since.

Jimmy continues to play music. He has found that a sober life has not hampered his musical abilities. Two years after this experience, he joined A.A. so that he had a spiritual community to support him in recovery. Now his music helps him to express his divinity.

I feel like I'm really part of the magic or mystery when I'm playing music-at least most of the time. I feel like I'm part of the whole. I'm a tool in the hands of the song. I get lost in the song. Once I asked a friend how did he handle being in this business that is so much about ego and still be on a spiritual path. He said, "Serve the song." If I'm serving the song, I'm part of this thing that is bigger than I am. Another very talented musician I know is not in recovery and has a serious problem showing up where he needs to be. He thinks that drinking, being a crackhead and being a songwriter all go together. What he doesn't realize is that songwriting is the antidote to your pain.

Make it work for you:

Try taking a class in any of the arts. Don't worry about how well you do. It's not a competition. Do it for the sheer joy of it. Or don't bother with a class, just go buy yourself a box of watercolors, oil pastels, even crayons and a pad. Or write in a journal every morning. Or try your hand at poetry. Here are some poetry exercises to get you thinking creatively.

1. Look in the mirror. Write a self-portrait. What do your features tell others about the person behind the face?

2. What makes you angry? Let it out on a piece of paper. Don't worry about whether it rhymes.

3. Look outside your window and write a haiku—a three line poem of 5 syllables, 7 syllables, 5 syllables.

 For example:
> Bright yellow flowers
> in big terra cotta pots
> shout out, spring blooms here

SEVEN
Forgiving Yourself and Others

One morning I had a strange dream, one which I knew meant something. I just couldn't figure out what. In the dream, my then-husband, an engineer who was not prone to emotional displays or sweet talk, was trying to tell me something "emotional." At first I ignored him, but he kept pestering me, saying he wanted to tell me how he felt about me. So I turned to him to listen. Then as he began to talk to me, a squirrel came up, pushed itself between our hands and bit me on the finger. I shook the squirrel off and realized there were several pesky squirrels around us, wanting attention. I was afraid that I'd have to get shots for rabies, but fortunately the squirrel bite didn't break the skin.

"Why don't we just kill a couple of them and then the rest will stay away," I suggested.

But there was another squirrel there—a golden squirrel with long golden fur. Someone entered the dream and explained to me that this was a rare squirrel from Alaska or some such place, and you certainly couldn't kill the golden squirrel.

Then I woke up. There are some dreams that are just dreams—your mind doing its strange drunken thing. Other times you are soul-flying. And then there is the dream that is trying to tell you something. Those are the dreams I remember clearly, the ones that linger all day. This was one of those. Usually I can interpret these dreams pretty quickly, but this one stumped me. Squirrels? What could they possibly represent? Especially the golden one.

I took my daughter to a friend's house that morning. They were heading off to camp for a week. A week without my daughter. I knew there was a dark cloud looming ahead, but I'd just let it rain on me until she came back and brought the sun with her.

"What should I do for junior church?" I asked her on the way to the friend's house.

"I don't know," she said. She was usually my helper, and we'd come up with crafts to demonstrate some spiritual idea. But today her mind was on her friends, on the camp she loved, on riding horses and swinging on ropes.

They left for camp, and I left for church. A forgiveness seminar had been scheduled for after church, and I was looking forward to it. I could think of a number of people I needed to forgive—an ex-husband, my father, my step-father, the woman who nearly ran me down in her SUV a few nights earlier.

But first I had to come up with ideas for junior church. Maybe there won't be any kids, I hoped. At first it looked like I was going to get lucky, but then someone brought her nephew. That would be even more awkward. What would I do with one kid for an hour? Well, I'd just have to wing it, I figured.

Our church is a diverse church. We have a nice mix of black and white, gay and straight. One of our African-American families often arrived with their four children. The mother was having problems. The father, I had heard, was a born-again drug-addict. The kids were sweet, but they didn't have boundaries. Tiko, the little boy, who was about nine, seemed to be 65 pounds of pure trouble. When I first met him, I had thought, this kid is going to be dangerous someday, but I discovered that this little boy, who talked about how he wanted to kill people or watch people get eaten, was just doing that little boy "tough guy" thing and that when he got some boundaries and positive reinforcement, he sparkled with goodness. Well, they showed up that day. And then two other children came in. Seven kids.

The session was haphazard, but fun. We took a walk outside and observed things with our eyes and ears. Then we went inside and drew what we observed and then added onto it from our imagination. We talked about our inner eyes and inner ears. We closed our eyes and told each other what we saw. The youngest of the children crawled up into my lap and gazed up at me with a rapt look. Tiko drew an awesome picture. He knew I was impressed with his talent. After service I taped it to the wall so everyone could see it. Then he hugged me. I was amazed at how much I cared about these children.

Then it came time for the forgiveness seminar. A woman had come from Nashville to give the seminar. The seminar contained a series of questions, triggers for people to feel old pains and hurts that perhaps they'd buried. I responded intellectually to each of the triggers. Yes, I'd been lied to. Yes, I had felt abandoned, rejected, whatever. But I wasn't touched. Other people began to cry, some of them to weep deeply. Sympathetically, I felt for them, and could occasionally feel tears welling up, but they weren't my tears. And then she asked the question: Have any of you ever had to agonize over the decision whether to have an abortion or whether your partner should have an abortion?

It was as if she unzipped me right then and there. The pain was as fresh as summer strawberries, as fresh as blood from a new knife wound. The babies, I thought. My babies. And suddenly the dream came back to me. The squirrels. How I thought that killing a couple would keep the rest away, and then the golden squirrel—the one I simply wouldn't, couldn't get rid of.

I thought of those children in junior church, the little four year old who had sat on my lap, Tiko's arms around my waist. My heart was like a ripe peach. I was filled with such love for children, and such pain for those I had never had.

The facilitator later asked us if we were willing to see the perfection in every situation? Could we be willing to believe that there was nothing to forgive. Yes, I was willing. I was willing to believe that everything happened for a reason, for a chance for me to grow and experience myself as Divine. I was willing to believe that there is no death, that those souls who may have been denied access to this world did not hate me, that perhaps they had found other, better portals or perhaps there was only one—the golden squirrel. And yet there was this pain. I had no one to forgive, not my father, not my ex-husband, not the woman in the SUV — all the possibilities I had brought with me. I had only myself and my recalcitrant pain to deal with. But how?

The first step was to feel the pain and to acknowledge it. I was not the only one who had responded deeply to this question. And when I looked into my friend's tear-filled eyes, we slipped out of our separation for just a moment. Our sorrow was the same sorrow. Our feelings of guilt knew each other. We were able to give each other the gift of forgiveness.

The truth is that we cannot forgive anyone else until we forgive ourselves. And once we forgive ourselves, we can eventually move to that place where we realize there really is nothing to forgive. (If you are interested in "radical forgiveness," a book by Colin C. Tipping, the originator of the workshops, is available, entitled Radical Forgiveness: Making Room for the Miracle. Or you can look up the Institute for Radical Forgiveness on the Internet for more information.)

Case Study, Deborah: Deborah is a 43-year-old professional who has dealt with eating disorders since she was 17 years old. She has been in recovery for the past four years and has discovered that self-love is the key to life.

Deborah: I never felt good about myself. I always had images of hurting myself, putting a gun to my head, stabbing myself, slicing my arms with knives and razor blades. I used to write "Fat Bitch" in ink all over my body so that I wouldn't eat. I was a devout Catholic until I was 30, but for a lot of that time I was also bulimic. I believed I didn't deserve to get better. Even when the priest told me I was a child of God, I didn't believe it. I might go a year or two without problems but then they'd always come back. I had to drop out of college because laxative abuse made me so sick I couldn't go to classes.

I used to pray to God to please make me worthy to be okay. Then I discovered that I've always been worthy. I just had to make the choice to be happy. But really and truly living that way takes work. What I am learning is how to practice self-love. The first step in that is self-forgiveness. I don't think I could stay in recovery without self-forgiveness. I used to ask myself, am I pure in heart? Am I pure in thought? Of course, I wasn't. And so therefore, I thought I didn't deserve to live. I lived in a state of damnation.

---------- Free At Last ----------

About a year ago, my mother died and then a few months later I broke up with a man I loved very much. I just felt so much grief and pain. I decided to attend a Radical Forgiveness Seminar. At that point, I was willing to do anything to get over the pain. It was very healing. You get together with people you don't know and you get to give away all that hurt and grief you've been carrying around with you. One of the things I needed to forgive myself for was an affair I'd had when I was married. Although my ex-husband had forgiven me, I couldn't let go of it for some reason. I kept beating myself up about it and it was impossible for me to stay in another relationship. I realized I was in a state of victimhood, but if I decide not to be a victim then there is nothing to forgive.

The question is, how? It's one thing to say I forgive myself, but how do you actually do it? For me, I show my self-forgiveness by treating myself well. I ask myself, How am I treating myself on a daily basis? In order to heal my self-hatred, I must be gentle with myself. For instance, I regularly get a pedicure, which is something I would never have done before. It's just a way of being kind to myself. I also started a dream list. I used to not allow myself to have dreams because I didn't think I deserved to live. But now I keep a dream list of things I want to accomplish in my life, places I want to go. And another thing I do now is that if I have an idea, I act on it. I don't just immediately shoot it down or allow anyone else to shoot it down. This has been great for me at work. Now, when I have an idea, I'll follow it all the way through, and amazing results have happened.

Make it work for you:

How can you show yourself forgiveness? How can you treat yourself lovingly?

Make a list of ten things you would do for someone you love and then do those things for yourself.

Look in the mirror every day and tell yourself, "I love you."

If there is someone you don't like, someone who really grates on your nerves but you have to deal with that person anyway, try looking into his eyes and silently say to yourself, "I love you. I love you." The transformation will be magical. You can do this mentally for anyone else you believe you need to forgive. Bring a picture of the person to your mind or look at a picture of the person and repeat, "I love you." Even if you don't mean it, try saying it, try feeling it, and keep at it.

EIGHT
Exercise & Nutrition:
Taking Care of Body and Soul

When I was in a drug program in Gainesville, Florida, one of the volunteers was a young woman who was a runner. She gave us some training on how to stretch before we ran, and she took a few of us out to run along the city streets. I didn't get into running very much (until I went to prison where I started running laps around the track), but I wish I would have started earlier. If I had known then what I know now, I would have turned to exercise in my times of trouble, and I am pretty sure my life would have turned out differently.

These days when life gets tough, I get outside and walk. The year that my daughter left for college, my marriage broke up, and my dog died (I know it sounds like a country song), I was as sad as I have ever been. I could not stand to be in my empty house, so I started walking around my neighborhood. I noticed that generally after 30 to 40 minutes, my depression would lift, and I would begin to feel okay again.

Almost any type of exercise is a more effective anti-depressant than you will find in your local pharmacy. I have used walking, dancing, bike riding, swimming and yoga, and they all do the trick. I took salsa lessons a while back. No matter what was on my mind at the beginning of the lesson, by the time class was over, I'd completely forgotten about it.

Exercise and nutrition are key to supporting your recovery. If you make a conscious decision to take care of your body and if you pay attention to the messages your body gives you, bad habits will fall away naturally and effortlessly. A sedentary lifestyle can be as destructive as any addiction. An active lifestyle, on the other hand, will improve your self-image, combat stress, and give you the energy to create an adventurous life.

Dr. John Ratey, a clinical associate professor of psychiatry at Harvard and author of *Spark: The Revolutionary New Science of Exercise and the Brain* has found a correlation between exercise and healthy brain function. He has identified "brain-derived neurotrophic factor, or BDNF, a protein that builds and maintains the brain's cell circuitry." His research shows that exercise helps you think better. And if you're thinking better, then you're less likely to make bad choices.

Studies have shown that kids who play sports in school are less likely to use drugs. And ordinary kids who simply engage in some type of vigorous exercise, such as running on treadmill or using a stairmaster, have shown dramatic improvements in their grades and their behavior.

Even in adults, exercise helps improve self-esteem and body image. It's easy when we feel bad about ourselves to smoke, drink, and eat too much. But if you feel good about yourself, that urge can be overcome. One of the hardest things about giving up our addictions is the loss of our identity as an addict. Exercising and eating well gives you a new identity, a new healthy image of yourself.

While there are athletes who do drugs and drink excessively, they don't usually last. They don't play their best when they're high or hungover, and they often get into legal trouble. And you don't have to be an athlete or be involved in team sports to get the most out of exercise.

Ratey and others recommend getting a heart rate monitor so that the only competition is with yourself. If you exercise (walking, running, cycling, etc.) in the 50 to 60 percent zone of your maximum heart rate, you will begin seeing results. Try to exercise five to six times a week for an hour a day. But start where you are comfortable. Maybe you start with ten minutes a day and gradually increase the time. You can also break it up. You can walk thirty minutes in the morning and thirty minutes in the evening. You'll be amazed how much better you'll feel.

If you want to lose weight, then you can elevate your heart rate. There are plenty of great books and websites that will guide you to becoming more physically fit. One of my favorite books is *Younger Next*

Year: A Guide to Living Like 50 Until You're 80 and Beyond, by Chris Crowley and Henry S. Lodge, MD (Workman Publishing). As we age some of the damage we did to our bodies may come back to haunt us. This book shows how to undo that damage and live better than ever before.

Eating Well

In this culture and many others, we are obsessive about food. We eat too much and then we stop eating and then we start eating too much again. We binge, we purge, we read every diet book we can find. We label food "bad" or "good" and then dream about the "bad' food.

For people who are compulsive eaters, Overeaters Anonymous is a great place to start. According to the OA website, "OA is not just about weight loss, weight gain or maintenance, or obesity or diets. It addresses physical, emotional and spiritual well-being. It is not a religious organization and does not promote any particular diet."

Some people in OA and other programs adhere to a strict abstinence policy, abstaining from foods containing sugar, high fat or alcohol. And there are people who swear by this. Some research suggests that a strict abstinence program may not work for everyone though. Sometimes when we deprive ourselves of foods we like, we wind up binging later on.

Here are a few guidelines for healthy eating:

- Eat breakfast! Not necessarily pancakes and bacon every morning, but something like oatmeal or a bran cereal with fruit will fill you up without filling you out.
- Get enough sleep. When you're tired, you tend to eat more to get energy. Then you also don't exercise because you're too tired.
- Unless you feel that abstinence is the only way you'll solve your eating compulsion, don't deprive yourself of the things you like, just don't have them all the time. If you like pizza, save it for Saturday night. If you like desserts, save them for special occasions.
- Organic, locally grown food generally tastes better, is better for you, and is better for the environment.

- Don't obsess about food. Eat when you are hungry, but stop before you get full. Give your stomach time to realize it's got food inside it. (Getting outside for exercise will help you avoid constant nibbling.)
- Don't buy food you know you can't resist. If that bag of Oreos is not in your cupboard, you won't wake up in the middle of the night and finish it off in fifteen minutes.
- Be careful of fasting. Fasting can send a signal to your body that it should store food and not burn energy. That doesn't mean you should never fast. If you want to fast for spiritual reasons, then by all means do so. But just be aware that too much fasting will confuse your metabolism.

Those are probably enough guidelines. Your body knows what is good for it. Trust it. I prefer a mostly vegetarian diet for a variety of reasons. But I know that's not realistic for everyone. Start slowly. Make gradual changes. Pay attention but don't obsess. Fruits and vegetables are obviously better for you than donuts and ice cream. So just use a little common sense, and if that doesn't work, see a doctor or join a support group.

When you take care of your body, you are providing a good place for your soul. You will be less prone to depression, you will have more energy for adventure, and you will be preparing yourself for the next step: total transformation.

Case Study, Richard: Richard was overweight, out of shape and on three types of medication. When his wife told him she wanted a divorce, he realized he needed to reclaim his life.

Talking Heads have a great song that goes, "I was born in a house with the television always on…" Most kids born in America in the 50s and 60s were born into that house, and I think that most of the boomers bought into the primary message of the television, that the purpose of life is immediate, effortless pleasure and comfort. A full life was one lived on a couch, guzzling soft drinks and snacks, living vicariously through people who were impossibly strong and beautiful, who solved all problems within either 30 or 60 minutes while the frozen meals were cooked, and clothes, dishes, cars, were all washed instantly and automatically, leaving more time to watch more television.

And if TV wasn't enough, radio provided a superb sound track in that era; magazines invited girls to romance with David Cassidy and boys to uncommitted sex with any number of exquisite airbrushed beauties. Was there a temptation to let the human side of yourself wither away, while all joy was centered outside in things you could buy -- cars, stereos, drugs, whatever it took? Yes. There was.

After I'd grown up and settled down, I married and gave up all the vices that society frowned on; I steered clear of drugs except those that the television endorsed. Every day started with a pot of coffee and half a pack of cigarettes before I left the house. Since I taught college English in the days when you could smoke up your own office as much as you wanted, the coffee and cigs continued as I graded papers, met with students, and planned classes. Working my way through three packs of cigarettes, the day would slow down with beers and smokes with my colleagues after work, then wind up with scotch and smokes into the late night while I wrote, planned classes, listened to music, watched TV until I went off to a happy, sound sleep. Somewhere in the middle was some regular food - pizza, a Quarter Pounder with Cheese ™, a slab of cow meat and baked potato with butter and sour cream. I loved that life and it created no tension in the home because my wife at the time enjoyed the beer, ciggies, and passive, sedentary, over-fed routine as much as I did.

The numbness of all that, and the fact that my jeans were 10 sizes larger than they'd once been, didn't really bother me, because I was quite well medicated. In the way that one bad habit usually attracts others, the coffee, smokes, and alcohol led to prescription drugs -- Benicar for high blood pressure, Metformin for diabetes, and finally Prozac, because I discovered my life lacked a certain exuberance at that point. That adds up to six different substances with their various side-effects that I was addicted to; together they seemed to be conspiring to kill me, and every one of them were sanctioned, actually promoted, by the television.

Then I got divorced, and for the first time in many years took a good look at my life. I had been sleep-walking through most of it, and I decided I was ready to wake up. I discovered that if I didn't have the two to three drinks on weeknights, I woke up fresher and more alert, and was able to get through my working day with fewer mistakes and less conflict, and less in need of a couple of beers after work to wind down. Without the slight hangover I'd gotten to think of as the "normal" way to wake up, I didn't need the coffee so much. And without the coffee, the nicotine wasn't as indispensible. It was like the bad habits were propping each other up, and every time I removed one habit, the next one, that it had been supporting, fell of its own weight.

Having the heart and lung capacity to take my 11-year-old canoeing held much more pleasure than any combination of beer, coffee, cigarettes, even antidepressants. I discovered that when I hadn't been smoking and drinking like a zombie, it was possible to actually enjoy swimming, hiking, even working out. And then one day I realized that 8:00 p.m. -- which had for a long time been the appointed hour to nestle into the couch with the remote and all 114 cable channels to keep me company until I dropped into my well-deserved sleep -- could be an even better time to put on the sneakers and leave the house on foot to walk for an hour, taking the time to stretch the legs and actually feel the air in my lungs, smell the trees, listen to the sounds that surround us every second. The TV was no longer a mainstay of my life; neither were the cigarettes and the nightly glasses of scotch. The red meat was out of the picture too, mostly because I don't like to support a system that keeps cattle chained to feeding troughs right up until the slaughter. Maybe I was identifying with them for some reason. Along with the bad habits, I also shed 60 pounds, the high blood pressure that required one drug, the diabetes that required another, and the nagging sense of malaise that went along with the rest of it. Six bad habits, seven counting the TV, that were trying to kill me. Now they're not going to get to.

Make it work for you

This one is really easy. Get up tomorrow morning and walk for fifteen minutes. At lunch time, walk for another fifteen minutes. In the evening, walk for another fifteen minutes. Do this every day (or almost every day) for a month. If you skip a day, don't worry, just start over the next day. Then add some minutes to your walks.

When possible, take the stairs instead of an elevator. Join a health club and learn how to use the machines. Take a yoga class, a salsa class, or kayaking. Try a variety of different exercise regimes so you don't get bored.

NINE
Open Yourself to Total Transformation

*"Man cannot discover new oceans unless he
has courage to lose sight of the shore."*
-- Thomas LaMance

When I was in prison, I sang in the prison choir for the simple reason that occasionally the choir got to leave the prison grounds. I joined right after watching the choir members trot out through the double gates for a Christmas concert. When Easter rolled around, I was overjoyed to discover that the choir was going out for another field trip and this time I would be with them. We got on an old white bus with bars on the windows and traveled to Ocala, Florida, where we had been invited to sing at a predominantly black church. I was thrilled to be there. The women wore bright clothes and extravagant hats. Everyone smiled at us and treated us as if we were their most honored guests.

We sang "Morning has Broken" and the church choir sang a robust gospel song. Then the minister delivered his sermon. I can't remember what he said. Only that his words sounded like song and he invoked the name of Jesus Christ with a dancing jolt of his body. Then I experienced something for which I was completely unprepared. The entire congregation had formed a giant circle in the church. And we were all holding hands. Suddenly wham, something powerful and unnamable filled every cell of my body and beyond. It was grace. And it was amazing. I was filled with an immense joy for three days. It slowly faded and then I had to deal with the fact that I was still me. I still had problems. I was an infant spiritually. And I had a lot to learn. At the time I didn't even know where to go to start learning.

I have spent the two plus decades since that day transforming, evolving, opening up like the lotus flower and sometimes closing back up and being angry and all those things I don't like. But I know what I desire above all else—that feeling of unity and love that I felt on that Easter Sunday.

Unfortunately, for most of us, even if we have a transcendent experience of the Divine, there is no shortcut to total transformation. Like anything else, it takes dedication. The good news is that as a former addict, you already know a lot about dedication.

The most important criterion is "willingness." Willingness means being open to life, love, joy, sorrow, pain—the totality of experience. As soon as you close yourself off to one aspect of experience, you start shutting down. Willingness allows growth. Without growth there can be no transformation. The opposite of growth is stagnation. Think of stagnant waters. The only thing growing there is mold.

One way to grow is to develop a spiritual practice. In fact, it is probably impossible to stay on a spiritual path without a practice. While it is best to create an individual spiritual practice that fits your life, it can be helpful to learn about the practices of others. I was fortunate enough to be able to interview author and teacher Joan Borysenko about her spiritual practice.

In *Minding the Body, Mending the Mind*, Borysenko translates some of the yogic practices she learned into terms that are very clear for westerners to understand. And in *A Woman's Journey to God*, she describes the rituals of Judaism to which she has returned and from which she has found solace.

These two paths have been united in Borysenko's life. I was able to meet with her one day and ask her about her spiritual practice. She told me that she is often on the road giving workshops, lectures and seminars, but when she's at her home in Colorado, she begins her day in her meditation room which is just large enough for one person. In her morning meditation, Borysenko combines prayers and songs from a Jewish morning prayer service with Chi Kung (Qigong) and yoga.

"I actually wrap myself in my prayer shawl as I sing and say prayers," she said. "Following that I do what I call a body prayer, consisting of some Chi Kung and yoga. I do what is known as the bone marrow wash, or purification. This entails bringing the chi, or what I think of as the Divine Light, down into the body and washing out everything old. I feel that I'm gathering everything that is holy in the universe and bringing it into my body. Then I do three sets of sun salutes."

This morning ritual takes less than ten minutes. And then she meditates for fifteen minutes before ending the practice by singing. The entire process takes between 30 and 45 minutes. But she can shorten it when necessary.

"People are so incredibly busy that they think they don't have time for spiritual practice," she said. "But it doesn't have to take long."

During the day, Borysenko reinforces her morning practice with breath-work and by saying her mantra, especially when she's feeling frantic or stressed. She ends her day with a bedtime reconciliation ritual and meditation when the first thing she does is look back over the day and see where she might have done things she wishes she hadn't.

"I forgive anyone I need to forgive for that day, including myself," she said. Secondly, she recites a prayer, opening herself to the experience of Oneness, and the third part involves meditation on the angels.

"Then you pull down the light of the Shekhina, the divine feminine, like a blanket to protect and cover you," she said, adding that it was a wonderful meditation for children.

Other habits you may want to develop as part of a spiritual practice: honoring the Sabbath, living in the present, loving others and service. You might join a study group that is studying metaphysical texts such as *A Course in Miracles* or Eckhart Tolle's book *The Power of Now*.

In *The Power of Now*, Tolle relates the story of his own transformation. He writes that he spent the first thirty years of his life living in depressed state. One night he woke up with a feeling of dread. He'd had the feeling before but this time it was almost unbearably intense. He thought that his own existence was "loathsome." He felt, he said, a longing for annihilation, a desire not to exist. And this desire was becoming stronger than his desire to live.

"I cannot live with myself any longer," he thought. As the thought repeated itself in his mind, he suddenly realized it was a strange thought to have. If he couldn't live with himself, then did that mean there were two of him? Was there a difference between the "self" and the person who could not live that self?

According to Eckhart, he was so stunned by this realization that he stopped having thoughts. Tolle felt as if he was being sucked into a void—a void inside himself. Then the fear disappeared and he fell into that void. From that life-altering moment, Eckhart was transformed. He began to live in a "state of uninterrupted deep peace and bliss" for the next five months. Then he began seeking after spiritual wisdom and thus began the journey that led to his becoming a spiritual teacher.

Cheryl Simone was an Atlanta businesswoman who yearned for enlightenment. She tried everything and followed every spiritual teaching she could find but continued to feel unfulfilled until she met the Indian mystic Sadhguru Jaggi Vasudev. Sadhguru's systematic program of yoga postures and breathing techniques along with his innate wisdom have helped Simone and many thousands of others to lead more peaceful and bliss-filled lives. As Sadhguru says, when you are on an inner journey, it helps to have a living map. A true enlightened guru may be the map that will help you.

Case Study, Colin: Colin M. started drinking as a teenager. It was a family tradition. For twenty years Colin drank and drugged, working intermittently. In his thirties, he remembers visiting his friend Charlie, who was dying of liver disease.

Colin: "Charlie was a good-looking construction worker who weighed about 190 pounds five years earlier. Now he was 120 pounds and his skin was yellow. He looked like an old man."

The two of them were drinking in spite of Charlie's illness. That day Colin left and Charlie's mother took Charlie to the hospital.

Colin was in a heavy period of drug and alcohol abuse.

"It's like that Lynyrd Skynyrd song – suicidal but not man enough to die. It was four a.m. and I was in this dangerous neighborhood, yelling at the drug dealers. I must have had a death wish. That morning about seven o'clock I drove my truck into a tree at about 45 to 50 miles an hour."

Colin broke his sternum on the steering wheel, and the skin was sliced from half of his face. He woke up in the hospital, surprised to be alive. Five days later his friend Charlie died.

Colin returned to AA where he'd managed to find sobriety before. Something was different this time. An older man who had been sober 30 years explained to him that people sometimes get stuck in the first three steps. The man told Colin he had to do all the steps conscientiously before it was possible to realize the 11th step: "Sought through prayer and meditation to improve our conscious contact with God as we understood Him, praying only for knowledge of His will for us and the power to carry that out."

Colin faithfully did the steps of the program and he also began to seek out spiritual growth and understanding. He visited a meditation chapel at a local Catholic church and also began going to "Deeksha" meetings (Oneness blessings) at a local Unity church.

"The first time I went to a Oneness Blessing, I felt this strange ache in my heart region. I told the Blessing giver about it. He looked at me and said that was the heart chakra. He didn't even know about my accident but he said that I'd had a wakeup call from the universe. It was true. My accident was my last chance."

As he continued to meditate and go to the Deekshas, Colin began to experience a deep sense of peace and even moments of bliss. Sometimes they were fleeting, but other times the bliss was sustained. Colin also read Cheryl Simone's book and took yoga courses in Isha yoga. A college student now, he continues on his spiritual path.

"Self-knowledge without spirituality doesn't work," he says. *"Sometimes it's still hard, but the more you experience the Divine, the*

more you know that there is so much more to life than what drugs or drinking can do for you."

Steve Kube's Transformation

Following is a story that my friend Steve Kube sent to me about his transformative moment. I don't know if Steve's transformation helped him kick his nicotine addiction, but I do know that he quit smoking a while after he wrote this. Steve studied "A Course in Miracles" and that led him to his spiritual experience (reprinted with Steve's permission):

I met this helper along the way, best described as compassionate, helpful, easy going, (and hard headed too), who said things I knew to be true, but I hadn't heard often. It was always someone I knew to be somewhat special who ever said those kinds of things and I was always braced for them. Those niggling bits of truth you don't really want to hear again. The saying goes; "When the student is ready the teacher appears." I always thought that meant the lessons would be easy. Ready equals easy? Don't know where I got that belief.

"How do you know this stuff? Where did you get it?"

I have trust issues and need a full background of the source of these niggling bits of truth. Who are you to affront me with these bits of truth that seem to threaten? Who are you to shine light on the discards of my soul? Where did you get this?

"The Course."

"Oh shit," I thought. I don't need to be indoctrinated in anything more. My mind is already like a bone some big dog chewed on over and over. All gnawed and worn to a frazzle. Who needs more of it? Not me. Inside I thanked her for her honesty and let it slide.

I was sincerely glad she'd found comfort in the Course. "I'm happy for you," I said. I really felt that for her. Now that I think about it I realize I didn't give a passing thought to the idea I could get anything like that from any source outside of intellectual understanding. Seems the only comfort I get is from myself, and not much at that. I concealed my misgivings as best I could and left.

We met a few more times. I really wanted to know where her understanding came from. (and to get help with some tough stuff I was going through). "How did you get here? What presented you to me? Who are you to teach me?" Those niggling bits of truth were pissing me off big-time… Trust issues… Yet pain drove me in search of a resource of healing. (I figure eventually I'll take the tools she used and do it myself but we were making good progress together.)

The Course

I went to listen to a group discuss the Course. Nice people but they might as well be swapping corn bread recipes for all I could tell. Made very little sense to me. Okay, it didn't make any sense. I didn't see anything profound at all. I thought the estrogen level of the group was entirely too high.

I went on my way…. But the niggling truths already mentioned kept niggling at me. How does she know that? She said the Course, and I knew she read a lot and experienced a lot more than the Course. Shit. She's a grandma. She knows pain. She knows sorrow. She knows love and a whole lot more. She's deeper than she lets on. She knows regardless of any course. She knows like I know. She knows like I know a lot of people know. What's with this Course?

I try again. Same thing. Corn bread recipes amidst a gathering of wandering kindly souls. Lots of laughter though. It was light.

Weeks pass and I'm tapping my forehead as I work my way through "stuff" and I can't entirely dismiss the way she said "The Course." Once more I try it. I decide if I don't get anything out of it this time I'm giving up.

Looking back it was interesting how I had the notion that I was to pay attention to the others there and simply observe and allow how they would proceed, how they would process the info the Course presented. I just felt I was to learn something by appreciating how everyone is an individual, how we make our way on our own path. There was to be an honoring of each one of "the others." I didn't think twice about this. That was to be my growth for the evening.

Okay, long story short, I got something out of it. Questions I grappled with five months earlier were laid out that evening. I read on while the discussion continued. I had to remind myself to stay with the group and participate. I participated a little but failed to mention the really important parts that were coming through to me. I wanted to just read.

I bought the book that Tuesday night and continued reading when I got home. I read the How it came, What it is, and What it says and went straight to the Clarification of Terms. Makes sense right? If they have special meanings to the terms you should get that first. Otherwise you might not know what they're talking about. Good. Got that out of the way and had a pretty good foundation to get going on.

I'm reading the text and it is not speaking to me. It is singing to me. I'm drinking this stuff in like it's pure water and I'm dying of thirst. It's flowing, making perfect sense. Every hour I can spare I'm reading and it's making beautiful sense to me. I don't really care if it makes sense to anyone else, or if anyone has any difficulty with it, I'm loving it. The Clarification of Terms, I reason, is what is allowing it to flow for me. Without that I'd be arguing with it. As it is I'm going full speed ahead and drinking it in.

Friday night rolls around and something in the Course comes up against the fast flow. I'm brought right into a core issue. I see it. Yeah, I see it. I'm enjoying the flow so much I don't want to stop and mull it over. I want to keep it going! I read on...

I've passed page 110 and for some reason I jump straight to the manual for teachers. Something in the workbook had slowed down. I wanted to jump ahead, to get the understanding and go on, I didn't want to work on myself just then, I just wanted to take it all in. The flow was just too much fun, too right on to get stuck. It's all singing to me and I don't want the music to stop.

I had thought I was going to experience a lot of derailments along the way. The Course was supposed to be convoluted at times. I'd heard others say they sometimes didn't know what it was saying. Too many words and all. It was supposed to be weird like that.

I'd read almost two hundred pages so far and it moved like a fast paced thriller for me. The pace was incredibly satisfying. It fed me at the rate I wanted to be fed. Nothing stingy at all about what it offered. I was really being satisfied to the marrow on the reading thus far, then suddenly I derailed. I didn't know what was being said. I was off the path and wandering in the weeds.

No problem. Just back track to where it made sense, read forward carefully and look for the transition. I did just that.

There it was. Page 42 in the Manual for Teachers. A word used in a new way threw me off. It still didn't make sense but I moved slowly thinking it would be defined by the context it was being used in.

I was tentative about it at first. I didn't feel I had cheated myself in any way so far in my reading thus far by faking an understanding, and I didn't want to begin now. Somehow it was that important to me. Not like forgetting who some minor character in a spy novel is and reading on anyway, allowing understanding to come later, or letting it slide all together.

I was prepared to backtrack again in the reading, to go back even further if I had to. Besides the damn book cost me thirty-two bucks. I should get all I can out of it. I read a bit slower, a bit unsure. I thought I picked up on the gist of it but was unsure. I even went back to the clarification of terms but there was nothing there to help out.

Magic.

I got a sense of what it was referring to and followed that. At first I thought of magic tricks, of prestidigitation, sleight of hand. Thoughts expanded to include clever devices and inventions. I thought of gadgets and gizmos that delight or baffle us with their intricacies. Twiddly hand cranked egg-beaters we don't need but enjoy fooling with. Then came electricity and all the 'magical' things we do with it. Light-bulbs, motors, air conditioning, integrated circuits, computers, and all that. Hundreds of examples came to my attention. My understanding built up in my head and held together as I read, but I was ready for it to fall apart at any minute and I allowed that I might have to re-read this part yet again.

I finished the chapter with a rather solid feeling about it, but still with a somewhat tentative "Okay". Who knows? Maybe my ego was trying to dominate the understanding? I wasn't totally sure. The material wasn't coming at me as individual words or even sentences or phrases. It was like listening to a complete song, or one song after another. Individual notes didn't make sense. Stanzas alone weren't enough. I had to hear the whole song to appreciate it, to get it, to allow it to sink in as a complete concept. It has a flow about it and taking it on as a static study wasn't going to work for me.

I turned to the next chapter and found I wasn't through with this subject yet. The whole thing continued to hang over and around me as I put it together in some semblance of understanding. Did I get this right? I think I did…. I read on slowly.

Glimpses of 'grand' accomplishments of men, of their egos, of their drives to achieve, to master the world, or to dominate one another passed through my awareness. The Great Wall of China, the pyramids in Egypt and elsewhere in the world. I saw cathedrals with flying buttresses and uncounted stained glass windows. I saw monuments and buildings and the many ways we've built them. Ancient cities and modern sky-scrapers. Stone bridges, sweeping aqueducts channeling mountain water to Rome so many miles away. Trains and train tracks, tunnels through mountains, trestles spanning chasms, roads, highways, superhighways, freeways clogged with cars and trucks. Massive ships crossing oceans. Battleships blasting one another to oblivion. The Titanic sinking. Airships, dirigibles, planes of all sorts, then rockets, the space shuttle and fantastic space going vessels navigating the stars. Were the last of those images from the future or from science fiction movies and television? It didn't seem to matter in the slightest. They were all examples of people playing around in this physical universe, with matter, form, structure, in time. Past, future, it didn't matter a bit. My awareness expanded to include it all and more and in the process become more intimately aware of that which exists outside all that. Spirit. A sensing that beyond all this stuff we see, beyond all the tricks and devices, beyond the 'magic' we create to inspire or awe or overwhelm others with, beyond all the effects of ego drive is a source that remains completely neutral about it all. Nothing can overwhelm it. Nothing. Beyond the edges of all this, remains that. By expanding to the edges of all this I found myself on the brink of that. That empty peace that's always there.

I sort of teetered there on the edge of it and thought; Yeah. I think I got it right. I pondered it as it all hung there in space. I wasn't allowing it to sink into my body as completely understood until I was sure. I let it hang there in uncertainty, in suspended belief or suspended disbelief. An "I don't know, but I think I know" sort of space. I was sort of looking at the whole thing all at once just allowing myself to "get it", even though I can see now I was on the right track all along. It was still singing to me. It still had the beauty.

I was in my workshop at my worktable reading the book and these concepts that held my wonder were hanging over and around me. My quiet attention rested on the material presented through the Course and I read slowly on and my certainty that I understood took hold. It has to be this... I continued to read the rest of the Manual for Teachers while all these ideas floated around me and began to settle in.

This is where it gets strange. About ten thirty or eleven o'clock, I felt something akin to a fine-tooth comb of energy passing through me front to back and moving slowly downward through my body. I felt snarls and tangles and knots in the fibers of my makeup being smoothed out. The comb of energy went right through me. It wasn't like any dawning realization I'd ever had before. Besides, this was happening in really slow motion and it had a lot of energy about it.

My mind went quiet and I sat with the sensation as it progressed slowly, smoothly, evenly downward. The bulk of the sensation occurred in the heart region, chest and back, but it started at the top of my head and went down. For someone with big-time trust issues this is a fairly big deal. Maybe this sort of thing happens to others with regularity, but not me. It was rather "twilight zone".

I sat and wondered about it as it happened. Was I being touched by an angel? There was a sense of a presence there with me but I did not want to look up and see an angel or two performing some sort of Reiki on me. I guess I'm cowardly about that sort of thing. I kept my awareness on the sensation of it and on that moving image of a comb of energy. I remember wondering if I was making it up or imagining it. It didn't change. Shifting my eyes side to side didn't change it either. I watched to see what it would do.

Was it a deep realization dawning on me at the level of heart and mind? Does this happen to other people reading this material? I was enjoying the sensation and didn't really want to question it so much. It felt good and I trusted it. It passed through me and was over in a matter of a few minutes.

I wasn't up for reading more. Something was happening that was not "magic". I'd like to call it magic but something grander is calling me to grow into something grander where "magic" has a different meaning. I don't know what happened and I don't know if it matters at all. I liked it a good bit and it felt real and trust-worthy. I sat quietly with the experience for a while then went to bed. I lay there in darkness and knew who I am. Without modifiers… not a man, not a father, son, citizen of the US, human or any other subset of "I am". Just me. I am. And surrounding that knowing was a tranquility. I just accepted it and fell asleep.

I woke a few hours later and tried reading more but couldn't. I was in a quiet space in the wee hours. Asleep or awake, it didn't seem to matter. That bit about magic and ego accomplishments had me wondering about aligning my will to a larger will. Somehow harmonizing with a deeper rhythm. Some bigger purpose… I closed my eyes and went back to sleep.

Saturday I planted irises and sensed what it is they prefer. I guess I tuned in to a will beyond my own. The BIG WILL? The will of the Big Guy? I don't know. Just the will of the irises today. They like a lot of sun. Plant them in the shade and they end up growing at odd angles to reach the full sun. They like their bulbs planted almost on the surface, the irises do. The vinca likes shade. Day-lilies like a lot of sun but a good deal more water than the irises.

Today I have the idea these are all instances of the will of God and I'm wondering what it would be like to find my harmony with the will of God. What it is that would allow me to grow so effortlessly as the flowers, trees and such. Where do I belong? What purposes have I? Am I on the *right planet? I'm just sort of quiet with all this in my mind and appreciating things as they are.*

This is Easter Sunday. The fine tooth comb went slowly through me two nights ago. A dozen relatives gathered for dinner today and I felt a great peace the whole time. I held a seven week old Matthew in my arms for a long while and swayed gently to the sounds of my own son playing his music thousands of miles away and years ago and we were each so undeniably connected right here in the NOW. I wasn't overwhelmed with it. It just was and I was aware of it.

I'm wondering about the fine tooth comb incident. I got a pretty clear visual image of the comb of energy as it went through me. It was maybe four feet wide, maybe three feet front to back, (couldn't see the back of it). It was much bigger than you'd think it needed to be if it was some sort of dawning realization type thing. It went through muscle tissue and all. I was quietly observing it as it went through me. I wasn't welcoming it or resisting it. I was rather detached actually. I try to recall that sense I had of perhaps a presence nearby, to maybe explore that a little deeper, then I think, nah, leave it alone.

Make it work for you:

I do not profess to be a guru or to be "enlightened." But I do know that meditating, reading spiritual texts and studying the lives of enlightened masters all bring a sense of peace whenever I am in the midst of turmoil and help keep me on a spiritual path. Select a spiritual text and study it thoroughly. It may be the Bible; it may be the Bhagavad-Gita; or it may be the Teachings of Buddha. Study the lives of Jesus, St. Therese D'Avila, Julian of Norwich, Sai Baba, Mother Ann Lee, and Paramahansa Yogananda. Read the teachings of Thich Nhat Hanh or Mother Meera. Find spiritual teachers, question them, but do not abdicate responsibility for your journey. Ultimately, the Teacher Within will guide you where you need to go. Search, seek and you shall surely find. The main thing is: don't give up. And if you fall, pick yourself up, practice instant forgiveness and allow yourself to be completely free of the past. Move on. Love yourself and in so doing, you will love God.

The *Course in Miracles* text says: "And as your hymns of praise and gladness rise to your Creator, He will return your thanks in His clear Answer to your call. For it can never be that His Son called upon Him and remained unanswered. His Call to you is but your call to Him. And in Him you are answered by His peace."

TEN
How to Help the Addict You Love

A new wave of heroin and meth-amphetamine addiction, self-mutilation and party drugs have joined alcohol and nicotine abuse as parental concerns. How heartbreaking it is to watch the child you nurtured for all those years turn from a loving, happy girl or boy into the walking dead.

Many of the tools I have recommended for addicts are applicable for parents and spouses as well. When I speak to parents of young addicts, the first thing I tell them is to give up the blame and guilt game. It is a waste of their energy, and they need every bit they can get in order to help save their children. If you are a parent of an addicted child, you must forgive yourself for any mistakes you have made and promise yourself to let go of guilt. It's just like the flight attendants tell you on the airplane: you have to put the oxygen mask over your own face before you can help anyone else. So stop beating yourself up. Love yourself. Tell yourself you are worthy of happiness, respect and peace. In order to love your child as yourself, you must love yourself.

There is only one cure for addiction and that is love. Now, I know you may be thinking, "No one could possibly love anyone more than I love my child." And that is true. I know that you love your child. The trick, however, is to remember the truth about your child and to continue to remind him or her of the truth. Your child is a magnificent and glorious child of God. But she has forgotten that. And sometimes, like when she just stole your wallet, it's hard for you to remember it, too. But remember you must. When you can, I want you to look straight into her glassy or bloodshot eyes and tell her: "I love you. I know who you really are. This isn't the real you."

My mother was not a particularly religious person. She found her spirituality, though she never called it that, through music. When I was going through my years of addiction, I don't think she even knew how to pray for me. But she did do one thing, and it is probably the thing that saved me. She refused to forget my true identity. She always told me, "This is not who you really are."

Your child is like someone in a coma. He may look like he's asleep, but somewhere inside, he is still conscious. He still hears you. You can't kill a vampire with a wooden stake. You can only vanquish him with love. Enough love and the vampire melts away and leaves behind the beautiful mortal he once was.

One of the reasons that addiction takes such fierce hold of young people is that addiction provides an identity in the crucial years when we're trying to figure out who we are. We cannot live without identity. Being an addict sets us apart. It makes us "special." Or so we think. As parents, you can help your child find a new identity. It's not easy. I'm not going to tell that lie. But keep the door always open.

For me, the new identity that finally worked was that of college student. Other former addicts have found their new identities through their work or through some form of artistic expression. Drew Barrymore was once addicted. Don Johnson and Robert Downey Jr. had serious drug problems. But no one thinks of them that way. They are movie stars—and they're clean and sober.

Your loved one doesn't have to become a movie star in order to find a viable new identity. And in truth this is not something you can force upon them. You can, however, encourage them in pursuits that might appeal to them. You just need to create a wedge between your loved one and the drug. Maybe he would be willing to try sports, the arts, some sort of job training or volunteering. Whatever the cost, it's cheaper than lawyers and rehab clinics.

If it's possible, get your child into a different environment. Is there a relative willing to let them stay with them for a while? Can you move? I know it sounds drastic, but I have seen such desperation in parents that I offer moving as a way to get free of those negative environmental influences. You and your child need to turn your backs on the past and on the people who would drag your child down. This is hard because not only does addiction provide identity, it also provides community. Your child will not want to abandon her friends. But she's going to have to.

As most parents of addicted and troubled teens know, a lot of programs just don't work. One of the reasons is that the residents in these places don't really assume a new identity. They're surrounded by other kids in trouble and collectively their old identities become even stronger. They're the "outcasts," which is better than having no identity at all. Of course, some programs are successful for some people.

One type of program that has shown some success is a wilderness program, which is described in the book Surviving Ophelia. Trudy was a single mother, whose daughter Karen caused her grief and heartache until she finally tried a wilderness program. Karen had become addicted to alcohol by the time she was sixteen years old. She also used drugs, was sexually promiscuous and engaged in petty crimes. The worst thing for Trudy was witnessing Karen's self-mutilation and suicidal tendencies. Finally, Trudy found a wilderness program that "felt right." For Trudy and Karen, this was a program that finally worked. Karen "discovered many things about herself during the program and learned to focus on one problem at a time. In the past, she had become so overwhelmed by her many difficulties that she gave up easily, but the wilderness program with its concentrated 24/7 almost one-on-one assistance, helped her strengths emerge. . . No matter what lies ahead, I am confident that Karen and I will always have a piece of the mountaintop within us."

Till Death Do Us Part

So far I have concentrated on parents of addicts, but what happens when you are married to or living with an addicted spouse or partner? Is it possible for the relationship to survive? Not always, but sometimes the "tough" but steadfast love of a spouse or partner can actually be the compass that helps an addict find his or her way home. In the book News Junkie, Jason Leopold writes that the love he felt for his wife, Lisa, was the one thing that was stronger than his love for cocaine. With her parents' help, he went into treatment, came out and stayed clean. But sometimes a person is on a self-destructive path that you cannot stop. Only you can know when to unplug your relationship's life support system and move on. Ask your inner guidance system for help and trust that life is always working for good.

Case Study, Debbie: Debbie was in a relationship with Chuck for two years before she realized he had a drug problem. Chuck's mother had died when he was four years old, and his father had neglected him. Chuck channeled his anger into serious cocaine and alcohol abuse. When they got married, he promised he would quit. After seven years of Chuck's on-again, off-again drug use, Debbie thought he had finally cleaned up. Little did she know, he had merely given himself free reign to use cocaine as much and as often as he wanted. Three years later and with a newborn infant, she finally discovered he had a full-blown addiction; she was devastated.

Debbie: I met Chuck when I was very young. I was so innocent that he could fool me. I finally figured out he was using cocaine. I was one of those who would get mad and threaten to leave. None of that worked. Trying to shame him only made it worse. He had to hit bottom and I had to get out of the way and let him hit bottom.

When I realized that he had fooled me for the past three years, I made him leave. I told him that everything was his own responsibility. He had to find his own therapist, his own rehab, his own place to live. I withdrew for three or four months. I was angry, but I believe God used that anger to help him change himself. I'd been trying to change him for years and it didn't work. I had to get out of the way.

He did find a rehab and he went into it. At first he didn't stop drinking; he just stopped using drugs. But then after about four months, I noticed a change in him. He was less controlling, less angry, more patient, and much healthier.

During that time, I saw a therapist and went to some NA meetings. I found the NA literature and the Twelve Steps were really helpful. I've always been spiritual, but I never trusted God before. I probably got my idea of God from my parents. I loved my mother but she was a perfectionist. So I figured God was a perfectionist, too. The best thing that came out of the whole experience was that I had to form a new opinion of my high power. Now my relationship with God is stronger than it's ever been. If I don't connect with God in some way or meditate every day, I find myself slipping away and losing what I found.

I gave Chuck a second chance. I think he hated God for his mother dying. He has now developed a relationship with God. He prays now. He never prayed before. Never spoke to God until he got clean and went through rehab. He tries to meditate every day and he reads the literature every day. He has his meetings three times a week and his therapy. We try to go to church a couple of times a month. I don't know if our marriage will survive in the long run or not, but I do want to see who he is going to become.

Case Study: Lee was addicted to drugs when she met and married Kyle. She tried to keep her drug use under wraps but he figured out pretty soon what was going on. Kyle had alcohol problems of his own, but he had no idea what he was getting into as he fought to save Lee from herself.

Lee: You know, Kyle stood by me, drove me to the methadone clinic, never chastised me or called me a junkie or addict. He just took me for who I was and still am.

He would even borrow his friend's car and drive to the shooting gallery where I was using drugs and drag me out. He almost got shot more than once for doing that. One night I jumped from the truck and got bruised up, and he doctored me back to health. He had to have seen my true self even more than I did to hold on like that. Most men would have just walked away. He believed in me like no one else had and he fought for my life. I never had anyone do that for me. They all lectured me and then shook their heads and walked away. True love doesn't give up; true love doesn't stand by and watch someone commit suicide. Kyle took action and used all of his strength to help me get back to reality. I hated/ loved him for it. The drugs were reaching out for me in one way and he was pulling the other way. Thank God, my husband, with the help of God, won!

How we ever made it through those trying years I don't know. We both have a lot of gray hair under this dye, but we have each other and that is the most amazing thing to both of us. No one would have bet that we would still be together today. Like Kyle said, we have a bond that cannot be broken. The love has changed over the years and is not the love we started out with. It is a trusting, companion-type love where we just know that the other will be there no matter what.

When we first met, Lee was pretty straight up about her past. The things she didn't cover, I found out about within the first year of marriage. Since then there have been no major revelations that I didn't already know about. As we were dealing with her issues, we were also dealing with my issues and our issues. ...yours, mine and ours!

In the beginning, I tried talking and reasoning with her. I tried going along for the ride when she needed to cop, hoping to somehow keep her usage to a reasonable level and learn more about her world. I tried to let her know that I was there for her and keep her occupied with anything else to help keep her from thinking only about the coke. I finally learned the old saying "You can't trust a junkie" was indeed very true.

Things continued to escalate to the point where ALL of the little money we had was disappearing along with her for days at a time. Soon the few valuables we had were gone, including jewelry and even her wedding band. I didn't know what to do. I talked with any one I could and read everything I could to learn more. I was told multiple times to cut my losses and get out! The situation was taking an enormous toll on me physically and emotionally, I could not concentrate on anything, which had a negative effect on my job, but our little issue: the 400 pound gorilla we had. I dealt with the increasing stress and pressure by drinking more, which was like throwing gasoline onto the fire....instant asshole, just add alcohol...

--- **Free At Last** ---

Throughout all this time I still was in love with the person who was behind that veil of coke. I NEVER forgot who she really was and to me it was worth fighting to keep that wonderful person and help any way I could with love, tough love and anything else I could do.

Finally, after Kyle locked her out of their New York apartment and refused to let her back in, Lee realized she had to make a change. It took a lot of work, but eventually Lee kicked her cocaine habit. And Kyle eventually stopped drowning his troubles in alcohol.

ELEVEN
My Story

The following is a reprint of an interview with me by John Grooms that was published in Creative Loafing Magazine *in Charlotte (June 22, 2010).*

Reprinted with permission.

Going to prison was one of the best things that ever happened to Pat MacEnulty.

By the late 1970s, when she and some friends were arrested for breaking into a pharmacy to steal drugs, MacEnulty had been aching for a big change. A smart young woman from a creative family, she had grown weary of the dangerous, drug-centered subculture she'd coasted into five or six years earlier and now found hard to leave. Prison wasn't exactly the kind of change MacEnulty had in mind, but by the time she was released 17 months later, she had turned her life around 180 degrees.

Earlier this year, Dr. Pat MacEnulty, wearing a stylish outfit offset by short purple boots, steps onto the Story Slam stage to read from her work. She's the author of five novels, several children's plays, numerous essays and an upcoming memoir. Her reading style is lively, almost theatrical, a raised hand or a lifted eyebrow punctuating her straightforward, nearly journalistic style with dashes of emotion and emphasis. When she reads an excerpt from her first novel, *Sweet Fire*, in which an argument rages among young drug addicts, the audience is rapt, silent.

MacEnulty teaches at Johnson & Wales University, leads writing workshops, enjoys publishers on two continents, has her own website, and is every bit the confident professional. So how did druggie/felon Pat MacEnulty become respected author Pat MacEnulty, holding audiences' attention with her clear, rich prose? That's what this story is about.

MacEnulty grew up in 1960s Jacksonville, Fla., as part of an artistically inclined, New England-formed family -- a background that gradually gave her a detached view of the city and its Southern ways, as if she were in it but also standing apart. Her mother, a highly talented composer, musician and director, was married to a jazz pianist.

"They had a horrible marriage," MacEnulty says, "and he left when I was 3. Then, when I was 5 or 6, my older brothers -- my two big heroes -- left the nest." She missed her brothers terribly, but her mother, whose responsibilities included being musical director for Jacksonville's community theater, took her to rehearsals, where, she says, "I learned to entertain myself. I read books, I thought up stories, I had my own little imaginary world going, I got to play in the costumes ... I think a lot of writers are alone for long stretches of their childhood, and that's where they start developing their imaginations."

When Pat was in second grade, a man broke into their home and assaulted her mother. Soon, mother and daughter moved to a more secure neighborhood, but the school there was stifling and "felt like a prison." Before long, "I was an angry little kid. I started acting out in the sixth grade, and didn't stop till I was about 24," MacEnulty recounts. Such elementary school "acting out" as shoplifting and serial cursing eventually turned into ninth grade pot smoking and acid taking. Her mother had remarried, to a man who turned out to be a heavy drinker, so in the early '70s, Pat moved to St. Louis to live for a year with her political activist brother and his wife, an opera singer.

"I learned a lot, so that was overall a good year in my life," says MacEnulty, who based much of her most recent novel, *Picara*, on her experiences during that year.

She moved back to Jacksonville and high school, "and that's when everything went down," she explains. "It wasn't a bad school, but I had too many self-esteem issues and it all hit at once: sexuality, drugs ... All the cool kids were into drugs, and I had to be the coolest and outdo everyone else -- I had to be an overachiever, I guess [chuckles]. I was doing really well in high school, I made the National Honor Society, but I was already looking down the barrel of a gun."

She got into hard drugs, then, after high school, went to college, off and on, for four or five years, doing well one semester and then flunking the next. At the same time, she got involved with groups of fellow hard drug users, and moved with them around the country; once, at age 19, she helped smuggle heroin from Mexico.

"I was part of that whole drug-centered subculture, moved around to Miami, to New York, and then back to Jacksonville," MacEnulty explains. "I'd see my mother occasionally, but it was hard on her to see what was happening with me. I tried a couple of drug programs during that time, but they weren't effective, and I was never off drugs for long."

She and her friends started breaking into drug stores to swipe drugs, and finally she was busted. Later, those years would form the basis of Sweet Fire. "All of those people," MacEnulty says today, "either died or went to prison for a long time.

"At the time [of the arrest], I was really ready to change -- the way I was living wasn't fun, I didn't like the person I was, but I realized that maybe I could become someone that I liked." It was if she'd been waiting for someone to temporarily set her aside, so she could get her act together. And so, as she headed to prison in her early 20s, Pat decided she was going to become a different kind of person.

Prison life offered MacEnulty college courses, as well as the chance to explore a dream she'd had since age 12: to be a writer. She had been writing off and on during the drug years, and once in prison, she dove into the craft headfirst. "I also got involved in some self-help things, positive thinking, and helping other people," she relates, "and oddly enough, I got some respect there -- for once, I was actually a kind of role model rather than just following along. So that's where I started being who I really am ... I learned that if you took the energy you used to get drugs and applied it to something positive, it made all the difference in life. Even today, I'll think about taking that energy and that ability to obsess about something, and use it constructively, just go for it." She smiles and continues, "That's probably why I've churned out six books, 'cause I'm kind of an obsessive about it."

While in prison, she also had a deep spiritual experience while she and fellow inmates attended services at an African-American church. "I realized there's something greater than just this frightened, angry little ego of mine -- there's something greater and much more beautiful and something of it is inside me. It may not always be accessible, but just knowing that it's there changes everything. And that's been a basis of how I see things since then."

Once out of prison, MacEnulty completed her B.A. work at the University of Florida, where she learned much from one of her teachers, the writer Harry Crews. The legendary Southern author, whose gritty books pull no punches in their evocation of real life in all its joy and pain, encouraged Pat to use her hard experiences in her art. After getting her B.A., she moved to Miami, and wrote for television, which is where she met her future husband, a video engineer. Still wanting to pursue the literary life, she moved to Tallahassee and got her master's degree from Florida State, after which she headed to Ft. Lauderdale, where she worked for the Sun-Sentinel for a couple of years. She got pregnant in 1990, "and moved back to Tallahassee to get my doctorate, because that seemed a better fit for motherhood than freelancing. My husband joined me there and we went on to raise our child." It took almost five years to get the doctorate while being a mom and writing short stories. During that period, she began working on Sweet Fire, taking Harry Crews' advice to use her own history and experience to populate her novel.

After being turned down by American publishers, *Sweet Fire* found fans in the British publishing industry, and the tale of 19-year-old junkie Trish, who "fell in love with heroin, which had made life both easier and harder," was published by Serpent's Tail in London. Reviews in the U.K. were terrific. MacEnulty was compared to authors Lorrie Moore or Jane Hamilton, and critics marveled that she could create a likeable, engaging character who is also a drug addict, and lace the story with intelligence and humor.

Intelligence and humor are key elements in MacEnulty's fiction, from Sweet Fire to her current novel, *Picara*. They sharpen the impact of her straightforward, often cinematic style, and allow for quick, piercing pictures of complex situations and emotions. In some ways, too, Harry Crews is still at work, particularly in the way MacEnulty tackles hard, tricky situations head-on with smarts and humor -- as well as in her knack for bringing "ordinary people" to full, three-dimensional life, making them as interesting as most ordinary people really are once you get to know them.

In many ways, MacEnulty's own experiences are reflected in her view of writing itself. "I believe writing can be transformative," she says. "You can take experiences -- your own or someone else's -- and by writing about them in an artistic way, turn them into art, and make them something better, or something healing, or transformative; and that can work for both the writer and the reader ... I know that after reading some books, I've been changed inside, I've gotten a greater awareness out of them. I think that's what I'm trying to do, trying to open things in myself by writing, and I hope that happens to readers."

MacEnulty's story epitomizes, and puts a human face on, some of America's favorite adages: Pull yourself up by your bootstraps, trust in what you do best, find satisfaction in your work, make lemonade out of lemons. You could almost see her as an all-American success story a la Horatio Alger, except that folks who think in terms of "all-American success stories" usually aren't thinking of former heroin addicts. Obviously, that's something they need to rethink.

Bibliography

Following is a list of books or authors I mention in Free at Last:

Borysenko, Joan. *A Woman's Journey to God*. New York: Riverhead Books. 1999

Borysenko, Joan. *Minding the Body, Mending the Mind*. New York: Bantam Books. 1988

Burnham, Sophy. *The Path of Prayer: Reflections on Prayer and True Stories of How It Affects Our Lives*. New York: Viking Compass. 2002

Chopra, Deepak. *The Seven Spiritual Laws of Success*. San Rafael, CA: Amber-Allen Publishing. 1995

Crowley Chris Younger and Henry S. Lodge, MD *Next Year: A Guide to Living Like 50 Until You're 80 and Beyond*. New York: Workman Publishing . 2007.

Dellasega, Cheryl. *Surviving Ophelia: Mothers Share Their Wisdom in Navigating the Teenage Years*. New York: Ballentine. 2002

Dyer, Wayne. *You'll See It When You Believe It*. New York: William Morrow.1989

Foundation for Inner Peace. *A Course in Miracles*. New York: Viking. 1996

Emmet Fox. *Power Through Constructive Thinking*. New York: HarperCollins.1989

Hesse, Herman. *Siddhartha*. Translated by Hilda Rosner. New York: New Directions. Copyright 1951

MacEnulty, John. *Finding the Love. http://www.emanations.net/*

Marshall, Tess. *Flying by the Seat of My Soul*. Grand Rapids: Tess Marshall. www.tessmarshall.com

Ruiz, Don Miguel. *The Four Agreements: A Practical Guide to Personal Freedom*. San Rafael, CA: Amber-Allen Publishing. 1997

Rumi. *The Essential Rumi*. Translated by Coleman Barks. New York: Quality Paperback Book Club. 1995

Simone, Cheryl and Sadhguru Vasudev. *Midnights with the Mystic: A Little Guide to Freedom and Bliss*. Charlottesville, VA: Hampton Roads Publishing Company. 2008.

Tipping, Colin C. *Radical Forgiveness: Making Room for the Miracle*. Marietta, GA: Global 13 Publications. 2002

Tolle, Eckhart. *The Power of Now*. Vancouver: Namaste. 1999

Following are some books about addiction and/or spirituality:

Soul Steps...Power Stepping to Recovery by Jude A. Allbright. Allbright's book presents an alternative to the traditional 12-step program, approaching addictions from a position of "Soul Power," rather than from the traditional belief of "powerlessness."

Changing for Good: A Revolutionary Six-Stage Program for Overcoming Bad Habits and Moving Your Life Positively Forward, by James O Prochaska, Ph.D. To uncover the secret to successful personal change, three psychologists studied more than 1000 people who were able to positively and permanently alter their lives without psychotherapy.

The Heart of Addiction: A New Approach to Understanding and Managing Alcoholism and Other Addictive Behaviors by Lance M. Dodes, M.D.

Under the Influence: A guide to the Myths and Realities of Alcoholism by James Robert Milam, Katherine Ketcham.

Addiction & Grace: Love and Spirituality in the Healing of Addictions by Gerald G. May, M.D.

The Pathway: Follow the Road to Health and Happiness. This book is about self-nurturing and putting limits on excess.

The Soul of Recovery: Uncovering the Spiritual Dimension in the Treatment of Addictions by Christopher Ringwald. This study describes the role of spirituality in a number of treatment programs. Ringwald sought out the stories of individuals from all walks of life who feel they have recovered from addiction through some kind of spiritual transformation. Ringwald also interviewed doctors, family members and counselors to understand more about the role spiritual belief can play in successful treatment programs.

Freedom From Addiction: Breaking the Bondage of Addiction and Finding Freedom in Christ by Neil T. Anderson, Mike Quarles, Julia Quarles.

Spirituality and Chemical Dependency by Robert J. Kus (editor) a collection of essays on each step of the Alcoholics Anonymous 12-step program focusing on how spirituality is used in recovery. Additional contributions examine chemical dependency treatment in the field of art therapy, and specific issues for gay, lesbian, and Native American populations.